GOODSON MUMBA

THE ART OF EDUCATIONAL LEADERSHIP

Balancing Vision and Management

Copyright © 2024 by Goodson Mumba

All rights reserved. No part of this publication may be reproduced, stored or transmitted in any form or by any means, electronic, mechanical, photocopying, recording, scanning, or otherwise without written permission from the publisher. It is illegal to copy this book, post it to a website, or distribute it by any other means without permission.

First edition

ISBN: 9798334414167

*This book was professionally typeset on Reedsy.
Find out more at reedsy.com*

Contents

Preface		iv
Acknowledgement		vi
Dedication		vii
Disclaimer		viii
1	Chapter 1: Understanding Educational Leadership	1
2	Chapter 2: Developing a Vision for Your School	18
3	Chapter 3: Strategic Planning and Goal Setting	33
4	Chapter 4: Building and Leading Effective Teams	48
5	Chapter 5: Instructional Leadership	63
6	Chapter 6: Fostering a Positive School Culture	79
7	Chapter 7: Financial and Resource Management	94
8	Chapter 8: Leveraging Technology in Education	110
9	Chapter 9: Legal and Ethical Issues in Educational...	127
10	Chapter 10: Leading Change and Innovation	144
About the Author		160

Preface

In an ever-evolving educational landscape, the role of a leader transcends the traditional boundaries of management. The modern educational leader must possess a unique blend of vision and pragmatism, inspiring and guiding their community towards a future of excellence while managing the complexities of day-to-day operations. "The Art of Educational Leadership: Balancing Vision and Management" seeks to illuminate the path for those entrusted with this monumental task.

This book emerges from my experiences as an educator, administrator, and consultant, witnessing firsthand the transformative power of effective leadership in education. It is crafted to serve as a comprehensive guide for current and aspiring educational leaders, providing insights, strategies, and practical tools to navigate the multifaceted challenges they face.

The journey begins with a foundational understanding of educational leadership, exploring its scope, history, and theoretical underpinnings. We then delve into the essential components of visionary leadership, emphasizing the importance of developing, communicating, and sustaining a compelling vision for your school. The chapters on strategic planning, team building, and instructional leadership are designed to equip you with the skills needed to translate vision into actionable goals and measurable outcomes.

Recognizing that leadership is not a solitary endeavor, this book underscores the significance of fostering a positive school culture, managing resources effectively, and leveraging technology to enhance learning experiences. It addresses the legal and ethical dimensions of educational leadership, providing guidance on navigating these critical aspects with integrity and confidence.

Innovation and change are constant companions in the realm of education. Therefore, the final chapters focus on leading change and sustaining long-term improvement and growth, offering strategies to overcome resistance and evaluate the impact of your initiatives.

Throughout these pages, you will find real-world examples, case studies, and reflective exercises designed to provoke thought and inspire action. My hope is that this book will not only serve as a reference but also as a source of inspiration and encouragement as you embark on your leadership journey.

Educational leadership is both an art and a science, requiring a delicate balance of vision and management. It demands courage, creativity, and a relentless commitment to the success and well-being of students and staff. As you explore "The Art of Educational Leadership," may you find the wisdom and tools to lead with purpose, passion, and a profound sense of responsibility for the future of education.

Together, let us strive to create learning environments where every student can thrive, every teacher can grow, and every community can prosper.

Sincerely,
Goodson Mumba

Acknowledgement

I would like to eternally and gratefully acknowledge the Almighty God for the infinite intelligence from His universal mind where we draw from all that we come to know and are yet to know. May I also acknowledge and thank everyone that has played a part in my journey of life in terms of spiritual, moral, emotional and material support.

Dedication

I extend my sincerest gratitude to my beloved wife, Edith Mumba, and our children, Angelina, Lubuto, Letticia, Lulumbi, and Butusho, for their unwavering support and understanding throughout the conception, writing, and eventual publication of this book, despite the sacrifices and challenges they endured.

Disclaimer

This book is a work of fiction. Names, characters, businesses, places, events, and incidents are either the products of the author's imagination or used in a fictitious manner. Any resemblance to actual persons, living or dead, or actual events is purely coincidental.

1

Chapter 1: Understanding Educational Leadership

Definition and Scope of Educational Leadership

Dr. Sarah Thompson walked briskly down the hallway of Crestwood High School, her footsteps echoing on the worn linoleum floor. It was her first day as the principal, and the school's atmosphere felt heavy with years of unmet potential. She could feel the eyes of teachers and students alike following her, their curiosity mixed with a hint of skepticism. As she approached her new office, she took a deep breath, determined to bring about the change she had envisioned.

In the afternoon, Dr. Thompson called for a meeting with the faculty in the school library. The room buzzed with low conversations as teachers, some veterans and some fresh out of college, took their seats. She knew this was her first opportunity to make an impression and to define what her leadership would look like.

"Good afternoon, everyone," she began, her voice steady but warm. "I'm Dr. Sarah Thompson, and I am honored to join Crestwood High School as your new principal."

She paused, letting her gaze sweep across the room. "I want to start by talking about what educational leadership means to me and what it will mean for us as a school community."

The room grew quiet, all eyes fixed on her. Dr. Thompson continued, "Educational leadership is not just about managing a school's day-to-day operations. It's about setting a vision, creating a roadmap to achieve that vision, and inspiring every member of the school community to strive for excellence."

She walked over to a whiteboard and wrote the words: **Vision, Strategy, Inspiration**.

"These three words," she said, pointing to each, "define the scope of our work together. Vision is our guiding star. It's the dream we all share for our students' success and well-being. Strategy is the practical plan that turns that vision into reality. And inspiration is what keeps us all motivated, especially when the challenges seem insurmountable."

One of the veteran teachers, Mr. Harris, raised his hand. "Dr. Thompson, we've heard these words before from other principals. How do you plan to make them a reality here?"

Dr. Thompson smiled, appreciating his candidness. "I understand your skepticism, Mr. Harris. It's true that these concepts can sound like empty buzzwords if not backed by action. That's why I want us to define our vision together, create a collaborative strategy, and build a culture where inspiration comes from our collective achievements."

She looked around the room, meeting the eyes of each teacher. "Educational leadership also means understanding the unique challenges and strengths of our school. It's about being both a leader and a learner. I need to learn from all of you—the ones who know this school and its students better than anyone."

Mrs. Lee, a passionate and experienced math teacher, nodded approvingly. "That sounds promising, Dr. Thompson. What's the first step?"

"The first step," Dr. Thompson said, "is for us to engage in open, honest conversations about where we are and where we want to be. I will be meeting with each of you individually over the next few weeks to understand your perspectives. Together, we will define what success looks like for Crestwood High and outline the steps to get there."

She concluded, "Educational leadership is about more than just leading—it's about empowering others to lead as well. It's about creating an environment where every teacher feels valued and every student has the opportunity to succeed. This is our journey, and it begins today."

The room erupted in a round of applause. As Dr. Thompson looked at the faces around her, she saw a flicker of hope and determination. She knew that understanding and defining educational leadership was just the beginning, but it was a crucial first step towards transforming Crestwood High School into a beacon of excellence.

Historical Perspectives on Leadership in Education

After the initial meeting, Dr. Thompson knew she needed to build a foundation of trust and shared understanding. To do this, she decided to delve into the history of educational leadership during her next faculty meeting. She believed that understanding the evolution of leadership in education could help the team appreciate where they were and where they needed to go.

The following week, the faculty gathered once again in the library. Dr. Thompson stood at the front, a series of slides ready on the projector. "Thank you all for coming back with such enthusiasm," she began, glancing around at the attentive faces. "Today, I want to explore the historical perspectives on leadership in education. By understanding the past, we can better navigate our future."

She clicked to the first slide, which displayed an image of a one-room schoolhouse. "In the early days of American education," she explained, "schools were often small, and leadership was typically in the hands of the teacher. These teachers were not just educators but also administrators, community leaders, and moral guides."

Dr. Thompson moved to the next slide showing a bustling urban school from the early 20th century. "As communities grew and the demand for education increased, the role of school leaders evolved. The position of the school principal emerged to manage larger institutions, and educational leadership began to formalize."

She paused, allowing the faculty to absorb the information. "Principals were expected to be disciplinarians, instructional leaders, and community liaisons. They were often seen as authoritative figures, focusing heavily on maintaining order and standards."

Mr. Harris raised his hand. "It sounds like those early principals had a lot on their plate, much like we do today. How did their roles continue to evolve?"

"Excellent question," Dr. Thompson replied, switching to a slide of a 1960s school. "Post-World War II, educational leadership began to shift again. The civil rights movement and other social changes brought new challenges and expectations. Leaders had to address issues of equity and integration, becoming advocates for all students."

She continued, "In the 1970s and 1980s, with the rise of educational research and new theories on learning, the focus shifted to instructional leadership. Principals were now expected to be not just managers but also instructional leaders, supporting teachers to improve student learning outcomes."

Dr. Thompson clicked to the next slide, showing a modern, diverse classroom. "Today, educational leadership is more complex and multifaceted than ever. Leaders are expected to be visionary, to manage resources effectively, to support and develop teachers, and to create inclusive, positive school cultures."

Mrs. Lee leaned forward. "So, what does this history mean for us here at Crestwood?"

Dr. Thompson smiled. "It means we have a rich legacy to draw from. We can learn from the past to understand the importance of being adaptable, responsive, and forward-thinking. Our challenge is to balance the traditional roles of leadership with the new demands of our time."

She concluded with a final slide, displaying the words: **Legacy, Adaptability, Vision**. "By appreciating the historical perspectives on leadership in education, we can better understand our own roles and responsibilities. We are part of a continuum, carrying forward the best of what has come before while innovating for the future."

The faculty sat in thoughtful silence, considering the journey of educational leadership through the ages. Dr. Thompson felt a renewed sense of purpose in the room. She knew that by connecting the past to the present, she had begun to build a bridge towards a brighter future for Crestwood High School.

Key Theories and Models of Leadership

Dr. Thompson felt the momentum building as she prepared for the next faculty meeting. She knew that understanding key theories and models of leadership would provide her team with the necessary frameworks to guide their actions and decisions. She entered the library, where the faculty had gathered once again, their curiosity piqued by the previous sessions.

"Good afternoon, everyone," Dr. Thompson began, smiling at the familiar faces. "Today, we're going to dive into some key theories and models of leadership. These concepts will help us frame our approach to leading Crestwood High School."

She clicked the projector to display the first slide, which showed an image of a man standing on a stage, addressing a crowd. "Let's start with Transformational Leadership," she said. "This theory, developed by James MacGregor Burns in the 1970s, focuses on leaders who inspire and motivate their followers to achieve extraordinary outcomes and, in the process, develop their own leadership capacity."

Dr. Thompson paused and looked at the faculty. "Transformational leaders create a vision, communicate it effectively, and lead by example. They foster an environment where followers are encouraged to be creative and innovative. Think about how we can apply this here at Crestwood. How can we inspire our students and each other to reach new heights?"

Mrs. Lee raised her hand. "So, it's about more than just giving directions. It's about creating a sense of shared purpose?"

"Exactly," Dr. Thompson affirmed, switching to the next slide, which depicted a pyramid. "Next, we have Situational

Leadership, developed by Paul Hersey and Ken Blanchard. This model suggests that effective leaders adjust their style based on the maturity and competence of their followers."

She continued, "In other words, leadership is not one-size-fits-all. Sometimes, we need to be more directive, especially when dealing with new or inexperienced teachers or students. Other times, we should adopt a more supportive or delegative approach, particularly with those who are more experienced and capable."

Mr. Harris nodded. "That makes sense. Different situations require different approaches."

Dr. Thompson moved to the next slide, showing interconnected gears. "This brings us to Distributed Leadership, which emphasizes the importance of shared responsibility. Under this model, leadership tasks are distributed among various members of the organization. It recognizes that leadership can come from anyone, not just those in formal positions of power."

She looked around the room. "This means we should encourage leadership at all levels, empowering our teachers and even our students to take initiative and lead in their areas of strength."

Another slide appeared, featuring a graph with an upward curve. "Let's talk about Instructional Leadership," Dr. Thompson said. "This model, which gained prominence in the 1980s and 1990s, focuses on the principal's role in improving teaching and learning. Instructional leaders set clear educational goals, manage the curriculum, monitor lesson plans, and evaluate teachers."

She added, "Our primary focus should always be on improving student outcomes. As instructional leaders, we need to be deeply involved in the academic life of our school, supporting our teachers in delivering high-quality education."

Mrs. Lee chimed in, "That aligns with what we discussed about using data to drive instruction."

"Exactly," Dr. Thompson agreed, clicking to the final slide, which depicted a diverse group of people in discussion. "Lastly, let's consider Servant Leadership, a philosophy where the leader's main goal is to serve others. This model, popularized by Robert K. Greenleaf, suggests that leaders should prioritize the needs of their team and help them grow and perform as highly as possible."

She concluded, "Servant leaders are empathetic, they listen actively, and they focus on the development and well-being of their followers. This approach can create a supportive and nurturing school environment."

Dr. Thompson looked out at the faculty, seeing a mix of contemplation and inspiration on their faces. "Understanding these theories and models gives us a toolkit for effective leadership. We can draw from each model as needed, depending on the situation and the unique needs of our school community."

As the meeting wrapped up, Dr. Thompson felt a sense of accomplishment. The faculty was beginning to see the multifaceted nature of leadership and how they could apply these principles to their daily work. She knew that with these frameworks in mind, they were well on their way to transforming Crestwood High School into a thriving, dynamic educational community.

Differences Between Management and Leadership

Dr. Thompson felt the need to clarify the distinctions between management and leadership in her next session with the faculty. She believed that understanding these differences was crucial for the staff to effectively navigate their roles within the school. As the faculty gathered in the library once again, she sensed their growing eagerness to learn and apply new concepts.

"Good afternoon, everyone," Dr. Thompson began, her voice steady and inviting. "Today, we're going to explore the differences between management and leadership. While these terms are often used interchangeably, they represent distinct aspects of guiding our school to success."

She clicked to the first slide, which displayed two columns: one labeled "Management" and the other "Leadership." "Let's start with some fundamental distinctions," she said. "Management is about maintaining order and consistency. It involves planning, budgeting, organizing, staffing, controlling, and problem-solving."

Mr. Harris raised his hand. "So, management is more about the day-to-day operations, right?"

"Exactly," Dr. Thompson replied. "Management ensures that the trains run on time, so to speak. It's about efficiency and executing established processes." She pointed to the "Leadership" column. "Leadership, on the other hand, is about setting direction, inspiring, and motivating people. It's about creating a vision and driving change."

Mrs. Lee interjected, "But isn't there overlap? Don't we need both to run a school effectively?"

Dr. Thompson smiled. "Absolutely, Mrs. Lee. We need both management and leadership to be effective. Think of them as two sides of the same coin. However, understanding their differences helps us balance our roles more effectively."

She switched to a new slide, depicting a captain steering a ship and a crew working diligently. "Consider this analogy: A manager is like the ship's crew, ensuring everything runs smoothly and on schedule. They handle the logistics, the maintenance, the navigation based on established routes. A leader is like the ship's captain, setting the course for new destinations, inspiring the crew to embrace the journey, and steering through uncharted waters."

Dr. Thompson paused, letting the analogy sink in. "Management is crucial for stability and reliability, but leadership is essential for growth and innovation. In our context, we need to manage our classrooms, schedules, and resources effectively while also leading our students and each other towards a shared vision of excellence."

She clicked to another slide showing a diagram with overlapping circles labeled "Manager" and "Leader," with shared attributes in the middle. "Great leaders often possess strong management skills, and effective managers can also lead. The key is to know when to wear each hat."

Mr. Harris spoke up again, "Can you give us some concrete examples from our school setting?"

"Of course," Dr. Thompson said. "For instance, when you're managing, you might be creating a detailed lesson plan, ensuring that all necessary materials are prepared, and that your classroom runs efficiently. Leadership, however, might involve inspiring your students with a powerful story, motivating them to think critically, or mentoring a new teacher."

She added, "When we had to implement the new curriculum

last year, the management aspect involved organizing training sessions, distributing materials, and monitoring progress. The leadership aspect was about rallying the staff, communicating the benefits of the new curriculum, and addressing concerns with empathy and vision."

Dr. Thompson concluded with a final slide, displaying a quote from Peter Drucker: "Management is doing things right; leadership is doing the right things."

She looked around the room, meeting the eyes of each faculty member. "As we move forward, let's remember to balance our roles as managers and leaders. Let's ensure we maintain the operational excellence of Crestwood High while also striving to inspire, innovate, and lead our community towards a brighter future."

The room filled with nods and murmurs of agreement. Dr. Thompson could see the faculty members were beginning to appreciate the nuanced roles they played within the school. By understanding the differences between management and leadership, they were better equipped to tackle the challenges ahead and lead Crestwood High School to new heights.

Role of Vision in Educational Leadership

Dr. Thompson could feel the growing momentum among the faculty. Their understanding of educational leadership was deepening, and she knew it was time to introduce one of the most critical aspects: the role of vision. She believed that a clear, compelling vision could unite and drive them toward transformative success.

At the next faculty meeting, held in the bright and airy school auditorium, Dr. Thompson stood before her team, a sense of anticipation in the air.

"Good afternoon, everyone," she began. "Today, we're going to discuss the role of vision in educational leadership. A vision isn't just a statement we hang on the wall—it's the beacon that guides our actions, decisions, and efforts."

She clicked to the first slide, which displayed an image of a lighthouse standing firm against stormy seas. "Think of vision as our lighthouse. It provides direction and ensures we remain focused, especially during challenging times. Without it, we risk drifting aimlessly."

Mrs. Lee raised her hand. "Dr. Thompson, can you share your vision for Crestwood High?"

Dr. Thompson smiled. "I'd be happy to, but more importantly, I want us to develop this vision together. A shared vision has the power to motivate and align us all. However, let me start by sharing some ideas."

She switched to the next slide, showing students engaged in various activities: collaborating on projects, performing on stage, and competing in sports. "I envision Crestwood High as a place where every student feels valued and empowered, where learning is engaging and relevant, and where we all strive for excellence not just academically, but in character and community spirit."

Dr. Thompson paused, letting the images resonate with the faculty. "A powerful vision connects emotionally. It should reflect our highest aspirations for our students and ourselves."

Mr. Harris leaned forward. "How do we make this vision a reality? It's easy to be inspired, but translating that into daily practice is the hard part."

"Great question," Dr. Thompson acknowledged. "That's where leadership comes into play. Our vision must be clear

CHAPTER 1: UNDERSTANDING EDUCATIONAL LEADERSHIP

and actionable. We need to break it down into specific goals and strategies, and continuously communicate it in everything we do."

She clicked to another slide showing a ladder with incremental steps. "Each step we take—whether it's improving our teaching methods, fostering a supportive school culture, or engaging with the community—should align with our vision. This ladder represents our journey toward making the vision a lived reality."

Mrs. Lee nodded thoughtfully. "So, it's about integrating the vision into our everyday actions and decisions."

"Exactly," Dr. Thompson affirmed. "Vision provides purpose and coherence. When faced with a tough decision or a new initiative, we should ask ourselves: Does this move us closer to our vision? If it does, we pursue it with full commitment. If it doesn't, we reconsider our approach."

Dr. Thompson then shared a personal anecdote. "In my previous school, our vision was 'Every student can achieve greatness.' We faced numerous challenges, but that vision kept us focused. One particular student, Maria, struggled with severe dyslexia. Our vision pushed us to find innovative ways to support her. With the collective effort of the staff, Maria not only improved academically but also gained immense confidence. By graduation, she was a school leader and an inspiration to her peers."

She looked around the room, seeing the faculty deeply engaged. "Our vision for Crestwood High can have the same power. It can turn challenges into opportunities and drive us to make a real difference in our students' lives."

Dr. Thompson concluded with a final slide displaying the words: **Vision, Action, Impact**. "Let's work together to craft a vision that inspires us and drives our collective efforts. In the coming weeks, I'll be gathering your input to ensure our vision truly reflects our shared goals and aspirations."

The faculty members exchanged thoughtful glances and began to discuss among themselves. Dr. Thompson could sense a spark of excitement and commitment taking hold. She knew that by grounding their work in a shared vision, they were laying the foundation for a bright future at Crestwood High School.

Challenges and Opportunities in Educational Leadership

Dr. Thompson knew that to prepare her faculty for effective leadership, they needed to understand the challenges they would face and the opportunities these challenges could present. This next session aimed to confront these realities head-on, turning potential obstacles into stepping stones for growth and innovation.

Gathering in the library, the faculty members seemed ready to tackle the next aspect of their leadership journey. Dr. Thompson began by displaying an image of a mountain range on the projector, illustrating both obstacles and the potential for high achievement.

"Good afternoon, everyone," she started. "Today, we're going to talk about the challenges and opportunities in educational leadership. Leadership is a journey filled with both peaks and valleys. Understanding this duality can help us navigate our path more effectively."

She clicked to the next slide, showing a list of common challenges: limited resources, diverse student needs, policy constraints, and resistance to change. "Let's begin with the challenges. These are the realities we face every day. We have limited resources, which can strain our ability to provide the best for our students. We serve a diverse student body with varying needs that require personalized approaches. We must navigate complex policy landscapes and sometimes encounter resistance to new initiatives."

Mr. Harris raised his hand. "Dr. Thompson, it often feels like we're just trying to keep our heads above water with these issues. How do we move from surviving to thriving?"

"Great question," Dr. Thompson replied. "It's important to acknowledge these challenges without being overwhelmed by them. Each challenge is also an opportunity in disguise." She switched to a slide listing corresponding opportunities: innovative solutions, tailored teaching methods, advocacy, and transformative change.

"Let's explore these one by one," she said. "Limited resources force us to be more creative and innovative. We can seek out grants, form partnerships, and leverage community resources. For example, think about how we can collaborate with local businesses and organizations to enhance our programs."

Mrs. Lee interjected, "I remember last year we partnered with a local tech company for a coding workshop. It was a great success and didn't cost us anything."

"Exactly," Dr. Thompson nodded. "Diverse student needs, while challenging, also present the opportunity to develop more inclusive and effective teaching strategies. By tailoring our methods, we can better engage and support each student, ensuring that no one is left behind."

She moved to the next point. "Policy constraints can feel limiting, but they also offer us the chance to become advocates for change. We can use our collective voice to influence educational policy, pushing for reforms that better serve our students and teachers."

Mr. Harris leaned forward. "And what about resistance to change? That's a big one."

"Resistance to change," Dr. Thompson acknowledged, "is perhaps one of the toughest challenges. But it also presents an opportunity for transformative leadership. We can use these moments to build trust, communicate transparently, and involve all stakeholders in the change process. When people feel heard and valued, they're more likely to support new initiatives."

She then shared a personal story. "In my previous school, we faced significant resistance when implementing a new student-led learning program. Initially, many teachers and parents were skeptical. We tackled this by holding open forums, listening to concerns, and making adjustments based on feedback. Over time, the program not only gained acceptance but became one of our most successful initiatives, empowering students and enhancing their learning experience."

Dr. Thompson concluded with a final slide displaying the words: **Challenge, Creativity, Growth**. "By recognizing the challenges we face as opportunities for creativity and growth, we can transform our school. It's not about avoiding difficulties but about meeting them head-on with a mindset geared towards solutions and improvement."

She looked around the room, seeing a mixture of determination and optimism on the faces of her faculty. "Together, we can turn our challenges into catalysts for positive change. Let's embrace these opportunities and lead Crestwood High School to new heights."

The faculty members broke into small groups, animatedly

discussing how they could apply this perspective to their daily work. Dr. Thompson felt a surge of confidence. By reframing challenges as opportunities, she had given her team a powerful tool to not just cope with, but actively shape their educational environment. This proactive, positive mindset was crucial for the transformation she envisioned for Crestwood High School.

2

Chapter 2: Developing a Vision for Your School

Importance of a Clear Vision

The following month, Dr. Thompson gathered the faculty in the school auditorium for a pivotal meeting. The focus of this session was to begin crafting a shared vision for Crestwood High School. She knew that a clear vision would serve as a guiding star for the entire school community, providing direction and purpose.

"Good afternoon, everyone," Dr. Thompson began, her voice resonating with conviction. "Today, we embark on a crucial journey: developing a clear vision for Crestwood High School. A vision is more than just a statement; it's a powerful tool that can unify and inspire us all."

She clicked the projector, and an image of a lighthouse illuminating a dark sea appeared. "A clear vision," she continued, "is like this lighthouse. It guides us through the fog and storms, helping us navigate towards our ultimate goals."

CHAPTER 2: DEVELOPING A VISION FOR YOUR SCHOOL

Mrs. Lee raised her hand. "Dr. Thompson, we've had mission statements before. How is a vision different, and why is it so important?"

Dr. Thompson smiled. "Great question, Mrs. Lee. While a mission statement describes what we do and whom we serve, a vision articulates where we want to go and what we aspire to achieve in the future. It's important because it provides long-term direction and a sense of purpose. It motivates us to strive for excellence and helps us align our efforts."

She clicked to the next slide, which displayed a quote from John F. Kennedy: "Efforts and courage are not enough without purpose and direction."

"Consider this," Dr. Thompson said, pointing to the quote. "In 1961, President Kennedy set a clear vision for the United States: to land a man on the moon and return him safely to Earth before the decade was out. This vision galvanized an entire nation. It inspired scientists, engineers, and ordinary citizens to achieve what seemed impossible."

Mr. Harris leaned forward. "So, you're saying that a clear vision can inspire and mobilize us, just like the moon landing did for America?"

"Exactly," Dr. Thompson affirmed. "A compelling vision can transform our school culture. It can inspire teachers to innovate, students to excel, and parents to engage more deeply. It can create a sense of community and shared purpose."

She switched to a new slide, showing images of students engaged in various activities—studying, collaborating on projects, and participating in sports. "Our vision for Crestwood High should reflect our highest aspirations for our students. It should capture what we want them to achieve and how we want them to grow."

Dr. Thompson paused, allowing the images to resonate with the faculty. "When a vision is clear and shared, it serves as a constant reminder of our goals. It helps us prioritize our efforts and make decisions that align with our long-term objectives. It also fosters a sense of belonging and commitment among all members of our school community."

Mrs. Lee nodded thoughtfully. "So, a clear vision not only directs our actions but also brings us together, creating a cohesive and motivated team."

"Exactly," Dr. Thompson said. "And it's not just about the end goal; it's about the journey. A clear vision encourages us to reflect on our practices, celebrate our successes, and continuously strive for improvement."

She concluded with a final slide displaying the words: **Clarity, Unity, Inspiration**. "Developing a clear vision is the first step towards transforming our school. It's about dreaming big and then working together to make that dream a reality."

Dr. Thompson looked around the room, seeing the faculty members deep in thought. "In the coming weeks, I will be organizing workshops and discussions to gather your input. Together, we will craft a vision that reflects our collective aspirations and guides us towards a brighter future for Crestwood High School."

As the meeting adjourned, the faculty left the auditorium buzzing with ideas and excitement. Dr. Thompson felt a surge of optimism. She knew that by emphasizing the importance of a clear vision, she had ignited a spark within her team. This shared vision would become the cornerstone of their efforts to create a thriving, dynamic educational environment for all.

Steps to Create a Compelling Vision

With the importance of a clear vision firmly established, Dr. Thompson wasted no time in guiding her faculty through the process of creating a compelling vision for Crestwood High School. Gathering them once again in the school auditorium, she outlined the steps they would take together to bring their shared aspirations to life.

"Good afternoon, everyone," Dr. Thompson began, her voice filled with enthusiasm. "Today, we're going to dive into the practical steps of creating a compelling vision for Crestwood High School. Crafting a vision is not just about lofty ideals—it's about grounding our aspirations in actionable goals and values that resonate with our entire school community."

She clicked to the first slide, which displayed a roadmap with four key steps: **Engage, Reflect, Dream, Articulate**. "These are the steps we will follow on our journey to develop our school's vision," she explained. "Each step is crucial and builds upon the previous one."

Dr. Thompson started with the first step: **Engage**. "Engaging our school community is essential," she emphasized. "We need input from all stakeholders—teachers, students, parents, and community members—to ensure that our vision reflects the diverse perspectives and aspirations of our community."

She continued, "Over the next few weeks, we will organize focus groups, surveys, and town hall meetings to gather input. We'll ask questions like: What do you value most about Crestwood High? What are your hopes and dreams for our school? What changes would you like to see?"

Mrs. Lee raised her hand. "Dr. Thompson, how do we ensure that everyone feels heard and included in this process?"

"Excellent question, Mrs. Lee," Dr. Thompson replied. "We will use multiple channels of communication to reach as many people as possible. We'll provide opportunities for both in-person and online participation, ensuring that everyone has a voice."

She clicked to the next step: **Reflect**. "Once we've gathered input from our community, we need to take time to reflect on what we've learned. We'll analyze the data, identify common themes and values, and consider how they align with our school's mission and goals."

Dr. Thompson encouraged the faculty to be open-minded and to approach this step with curiosity and humility. "We may uncover insights that challenge our assumptions or push us out of our comfort zones. Embracing this discomfort is essential for growth and innovation."

She moved to the third step: **Dream**. "This is where we let our imaginations soar," Dr. Thompson exclaimed. "We'll envision the future we want to create for Crestwood High—a future where every student thrives academically, socially, and emotionally. We'll dream big and think creatively about what's possible."

Mr. Harris grinned. "Sounds like the fun part!"

Dr. Thompson chuckled. "Absolutely, Mr. Harris. This step is all about tapping into our collective creativity and pushing the boundaries of what we believe is achievable."

Finally, Dr. Thompson clicked to the last step: **Articulate**. "Once we've engaged, reflected, and dreamed, it's time to articulate our vision in clear and compelling terms. We'll distill our aspirations into a concise statement that captures the essence of what we want to achieve and why it matters."

She paused, letting the significance of this step sink in. "Our vision statement will serve as our guiding light, guiding our actions, decisions, and priorities. It will inspire and motivate us to work towards a common purpose."

Dr. Thompson concluded with a final slide displaying the words: **Engage, Reflect, Dream, Articulate**. "Creating a compelling vision is a collaborative and iterative process. It requires patience, openness, and a willingness to embrace change. But I have no doubt that together, we will craft a vision that reflects the best of Crestwood High School and propels us towards a future of excellence."

As the faculty members filed out of the auditorium, Dr. Thompson could sense their excitement and determination. By breaking down the process of creating a vision into actionable steps, she had empowered her team to take ownership of their school's future. She knew that with their collective creativity and commitment, they would create a vision that truly captured the spirit of Crestwood High School.

Involving Stakeholders in Vision Development

With the framework for creating a compelling vision established, Dr. Thompson knew that involving stakeholders in the vision development process was paramount. She understood that their input and buy-in were essential for the vision to truly reflect the aspirations and values of the entire school community. Gathering the faculty once again in the school auditorium, she embarked on the next phase of their journey.

"Welcome back, everyone," Dr. Thompson greeted, her voice resonating with warmth and enthusiasm. "Today, we're going to delve into the crucial step of involving stakeholders in the development of our school's vision. Engaging our community ensures that our vision is inclusive, relevant, and meaningful to all."

She clicked to the first slide, which displayed a diverse group of people—teachers, students, parents, and community members—gathered around a table in discussion. "Our stakeholders are the heart and soul of Crestwood High School," she explained. "Their perspectives, insights, and aspirations are invaluable in shaping our shared vision."

Dr. Thompson emphasized the importance of reaching out to a wide range of stakeholders. "We want to hear from everyone who has a stake in our school's future," she said. "That includes teachers, staff, students, parents, alumni, local businesses, community leaders, and other partners."

She continued, "Each stakeholder group brings a unique perspective and expertise to the table. By involving them in the vision development process, we ensure that our vision reflects the diverse needs and priorities of our entire school community."

Mrs. Lee raised her hand. "Dr. Thompson, how do we go about involving all these different groups effectively?"

"Great question, Mrs. Lee," Dr. Thompson replied. "We will use a variety of methods to engage stakeholders and gather their input. This might include surveys, focus groups, town hall meetings, interviews, and online platforms."

She clicked to the next slide, which displayed a timeline outlining the stakeholder engagement process. "We will be intentional and systematic in our approach," she explained. "We'll start by conducting an initial survey to assess the current perceptions and priorities of our stakeholders. This will provide us with valuable baseline data to inform our next steps."

Dr. Thompson then outlined a series of focus groups

and town hall meetings where stakeholders would have the opportunity to share their ideas, concerns, and aspirations for Crestwood High School. "These sessions will be interactive and participatory," she emphasized. "We want everyone to feel heard and valued."

Mr. Harris nodded in agreement. "It sounds like you've thought this through, Dr. Thompson. I'm excited to see how our stakeholders' input will shape our vision."

"Absolutely, Mr. Harris," Dr. Thompson said with a smile. "Their input will be instrumental in crafting a vision that truly reflects the aspirations and values of our school community."

She concluded with a final slide displaying the words: **Engage, Listen, Collaborate**. "Involving stakeholders in the vision development process is not only essential—it's empowering. Together, we will co-create a vision that inspires and unites us all."

As the faculty members filed out of the auditorium, Dr. Thompson could sense their enthusiasm and determination. By emphasizing the importance of involving stakeholders in the vision development process, she had laid the foundation for a collaborative and inclusive approach to shaping Crestwood High School's future. She knew that with their collective input and commitment, they would create a vision that truly reflected the hopes and dreams of their entire school community.

Aligning Vision with School Goals and Objectives

With stakeholders engaged and their input gathered, Dr. Thompson led the faculty through the crucial step of aligning the emerging vision with the school's goals and objectives. Recognizing the importance of coherence and synergy between the vision and the school's broader strategic framework, she gathered the faculty once again in the school auditorium.

"Welcome back, everyone," Dr. Thompson greeted, her voice filled with anticipation. "Today, we're going to focus on aligning our emerging vision with the goals and objectives of Crestwood High School. By ensuring alignment, we ensure that our vision guides and supports our strategic direction."

She clicked to the first slide, which displayed a Venn diagram with overlapping circles labeled "Vision" and "Goals & Objectives." "Our vision is the North Star that guides us towards our desired future," she explained. "But for it to be effective, it must be aligned with the specific goals and objectives we've set for our school."

Dr. Thompson emphasized the importance of coherence and integration. "Our vision should not exist in isolation—it should be deeply interconnected with our broader strategic framework. It should inform and inspire our goals and objectives, and vice versa."

Mrs. Lee raised her hand. "Dr. Thompson, how do we ensure that our vision aligns seamlessly with our goals and objectives?"

"Great question, Mrs. Lee," Dr. Thompson replied. "Alignment requires deliberate effort and careful consideration. We'll start by reviewing our existing goals and objectives to identify any gaps or inconsistencies with the emerging vision."

She clicked to the next slide, which displayed a matrix aligning the school's vision with its goals and objectives. "We'll then map out how each element of our vision aligns with specific goals and objectives. This will ensure that our vision serves as a guiding framework for our strategic priorities."

Dr. Thompson encouraged the faculty to think holistically about alignment. "Our vision should not only align with our academic goals but also with our broader goals related to student well-being, equity, diversity, and community engagement."

She moved to the next step: **Integration**. "Once we've identified alignment opportunities, we'll integrate our vision into our planning processes," Dr. Thompson explained. "We'll ensure that our vision is reflected in our annual school improvement plans, budget allocations, professional development initiatives, and other strategic initiatives."

Mr. Harris nodded in understanding. "So, it's not just about having a vision statement—it's about embedding that vision into everything we do."

"Exactly," Dr. Thompson affirmed. "Our vision should be the lens through which we view and evaluate all our actions and decisions. It should guide our daily practices and long-term strategies, ensuring that we stay focused on our ultimate goals."

She concluded with a final slide displaying the words: **Alignment, Integration, Action**. "By aligning our emerging vision with our goals and objectives, we ensure that our school's efforts are cohesive, purposeful, and impactful. Together, we will transform our shared vision into a reality that benefits every member of the Crestwood High School community."

As the faculty members filed out of the auditorium, Dr. Thompson could sense their growing clarity and determination. By emphasizing the importance of aligning the vision with the school's goals and objectives, she had equipped her team with a powerful tool for strategic alignment and implementation. She knew that with their collective commitment and focus, they would turn their vision into tangible results that would benefit their students and community for years to come.

Communicating the Vision Effectively

Recognizing that a compelling vision is only effective if it is communicated clearly and consistently, Dr. Thompson led the faculty through the critical step of communicating the emerging vision to the entire school community. Gathering them once again in the school auditorium, she emphasized the importance of effective communication in bringing the vision to life.

"Welcome back, everyone," Dr. Thompson began, her voice filled with purpose. "Today, we're going to focus on the crucial task of communicating our emerging vision effectively. Communication is the bridge that connects our vision to the hearts and minds of our school community."

She clicked to the first slide, which displayed a communication plan with various channels and strategies. "Our communication plan will ensure that our vision is shared, understood, and embraced by all members of the Crestwood High School community."

Dr. Thompson stressed the need for clarity and consistency. "Effective communication begins with a clear and concise message," she explained. "We'll distill our vision into a memorable statement that captures the essence of what we aspire to achieve and why it matters."

She encouraged the faculty to think creatively about how they could communicate the vision in a way that resonated with different audiences. "We'll use a variety of channels and mediums—such as newsletters, social media, website updates, staff meetings, parent forums, and student assemblies—to reach everyone in our school community."

Mrs. Lee raised her hand. "Dr. Thompson, how do we ensure

that our communication is engaging and impactful?"

"Great question, Mrs. Lee," Dr. Thompson replied. "Engagement is key to effective communication. We'll use storytelling, visuals, and interactive activities to bring our vision to life and make it relevant to our audience."

She clicked to the next slide, which displayed examples of engaging communication materials, such as videos, infographics, and testimonials. "We'll share success stories, testimonials, and examples of how our vision is already making a difference in the lives of our students and staff. This will help people see the tangible benefits of our vision and inspire them to get involved."

Mr. Harris nodded in understanding. "So, it's not just about telling people what our vision is—it's about showing them why it matters and how they can contribute."

"Exactly," Dr. Thompson affirmed. "Our communication should be inclusive and inviting, inviting everyone to be part of the vision. We'll create opportunities for feedback and dialogue, ensuring that everyone has a voice in shaping our shared future."

She concluded with a final slide displaying the words: **Clarity, Consistency, Engagement**. "By communicating our vision effectively, we ensure that it becomes more than just words on paper—it becomes a living, breathing reality that guides and inspires us all."

As the faculty members filed out of the auditorium, Dr. Thompson could sense their enthusiasm and commitment to effectively communicate the vision. By emphasizing the importance of clarity, consistency, and engagement in their communication efforts, she had empowered her team to bring the vision to life in a way that resonated with the entire school community. She knew that with their collective creativity and dedication, they would ensure that their vision became a shared reality at Crestwood High School.

Sustaining and Adapting the Vision Over Time

Understanding that a compelling vision is not static but evolves over time, Dr. Thompson guided the faculty through the final step of sustaining and adapting the vision to ensure its continued relevance and effectiveness. Gathering them once again in the school auditorium, she emphasized the importance of ongoing reflection, evaluation, and adjustment in maintaining the vision's vitality.

"Welcome back, everyone," Dr. Thompson greeted, her voice carrying a tone of reflection. "Today, we're going to explore the crucial task of sustaining and adapting our vision over time. A vision is not a one-time event—it's a journey of continuous improvement and renewal."

She clicked to the first slide, which displayed a cycle of reflection, evaluation, and adjustment. "Our vision is a living document that must evolve with the changing needs and circumstances of our school community. To sustain it, we must be proactive in reflecting on its effectiveness, evaluating our progress, and making adjustments as needed."

Dr. Thompson stressed the importance of reflection. "Reflection allows us to pause and consider how well our vision is guiding our actions and decisions. We'll regularly assess whether our current practices align with our vision and identify areas for improvement."

She encouraged the faculty to engage in regular discussions and self-assessments to gauge the vision's impact. "We'll ask ourselves: Are we living up to our vision? What successes have we achieved? What challenges have we encountered? And most importantly, what lessons have we learned?"

Mrs. Lee raised her hand. "Dr. Thompson, how do we ensure that our vision remains relevant in the face of changing circumstances?"

"Excellent question, Mrs. Lee," Dr. Thompson replied. "Adaptation is key to sustaining our vision over time. We must be flexible and responsive to new challenges, opportunities, and priorities."

She clicked to the next slide, which displayed examples of adaptive strategies, such as revising goals, updating action plans, and seeking new input from stakeholders. "We'll regularly review and revise our vision to ensure that it remains aligned with our school's evolving needs and aspirations. This might involve updating our goals, refining our strategies, or even revisiting our core values."

Mr. Harris nodded in understanding. "So, it's not about sticking to a rigid plan—it's about being willing to change and grow."

"Exactly," Dr. Thompson affirmed. "Our vision should be a dynamic and responsive framework that guides our continuous improvement efforts. By staying open to feedback, embracing change, and adapting our approach as needed, we ensure that our vision remains relevant and impactful over time."

She concluded with a final slide displaying the words: **Reflection, Evaluation, Adaptation**. "By sustaining and adapting our vision over time, we ensure that it remains a powerful force for positive change in our school community. Together, we will continue to evolve and grow, guided by our shared vision of excellence."

As the faculty members filed out of the auditorium, Dr. Thompson could sense their renewed commitment to sustaining and adapting the vision over time. By emphasizing the importance of ongoing reflection and adaptation, she had empowered her team to embrace change and innovation in pursuit of their shared vision. She knew that with their collective resilience and dedication, they would ensure that their vision continued to inspire and guide Crestwood High School for years to come.

3

Chapter 3: Strategic Planning and Goal Setting

Importance of Strategic Planning in Education

In the next phase of their leadership journey, Dr. Thompson led the faculty through the importance of strategic planning in education. Recognizing the pivotal role strategic planning plays in shaping the future of Crestwood High School, she gathered the faculty once again in the school auditorium.

"Good morning, everyone," Dr. Thompson began, her voice projecting authority and purpose. "Today, we embark on a crucial aspect of educational leadership: strategic planning. Strategic planning is not just a bureaucratic exercise—it's the compass that guides our school's journey towards excellence."

She clicked to the first slide, which displayed a mountain peak symbolizing success, with a winding path leading towards it. "Just like climbers need a map and compass to reach the summit, schools need a strategic plan to navigate the complex terrain of education."

Dr. Thompson emphasized the importance of foresight and intentionality. "Strategic planning allows us to anticipate challenges, leverage opportunities, and chart a course for success. It ensures that our efforts are focused, coherent, and aligned with our long-term vision and goals."

She continued, "In today's rapidly changing educational landscape, strategic planning is more important than ever. It enables us to adapt to new realities, innovate in our practices, and stay ahead of the curve."

Mr. Harris raised his hand. "Dr. Thompson, how does strategic planning help us address the unique needs of our students and community?"

"Great question, Mr. Harris," Dr. Thompson replied. "Strategic planning provides a framework for addressing the diverse needs and aspirations of our stakeholders. By engaging in a systematic process of goal setting and priority setting, we can ensure that our resources are allocated effectively and that our initiatives are aligned with our mission and vision."

She clicked to the next slide, which displayed a diagram illustrating the components of strategic planning: analysis, goal setting, action planning, implementation, and evaluation. "Strategic planning involves a series of interconnected steps that guide our decision-making and resource allocation. Each step is essential for ensuring that our efforts are focused, purposeful, and impactful."

Dr. Thompson encouraged the faculty to embrace strategic planning as a collaborative process. "Strategic planning is not something we do in isolation—it requires the input and engagement of all stakeholders. By involving teachers, students, parents, and community members in the process, we ensure that our strategic plan reflects the diverse perspectives and priorities of our school community."

She concluded with a final slide displaying the words: **Foresight, Intentionality, Collaboration**. "By embracing strategic planning, we can ensure that Crestwood High School remains at the forefront of educational excellence. Together, we will chart a course for success that benefits every member of our school community."

As the faculty members filed out of the auditorium, Dr. Thompson could sense their growing appreciation for the importance of strategic planning in education. By emphasizing the role of strategic planning as a guiding compass for their school's journey, she had empowered her team to approach the task with clarity, purpose, and collaboration. She knew that with their collective commitment and effort, they would develop a strategic plan that set Crestwood High School on a path towards even greater success and impact.

Components of a Strategic Plan

With the importance of strategic planning firmly established, Dr. Thompson guided the faculty through the essential components of a strategic plan. Understanding that a well-crafted plan serves as a roadmap for achieving their school's vision and goals, she gathered the faculty once again in the school auditorium.

"Welcome back, everyone," Dr. Thompson greeted, her voice filled with purpose. "Today, we're going to delve into the essential components of a strategic plan. A strategic plan is not just a document—it's a blueprint for our school's future success."

She clicked to the first slide, which displayed a roadmap with key components labeled: **Mission, Vision, Goals, Objectives, Strategies, Action Plans, Monitoring & Evaluation**. "These are the building blocks of our strategic plan," she explained. "Each component plays a critical role in guiding our school's direction and priorities."

Dr. Thompson started with the foundation: **Mission** and **Vision**. "Our mission and vision statements capture the core purpose and aspirations of our school," she said. "They define who we are, what we stand for, and where we're headed. Our mission is our reason for being, while our vision is our desired future state."

She emphasized the importance of clarity and alignment. "Our mission and vision statements should be concise, inspiring, and reflective of our values and priorities. They provide the guiding framework for everything we do."

Mrs. Lee raised her hand. "Dr. Thompson, how do we ensure that our mission and vision statements resonate with our stakeholders?"

"Excellent question, Mrs. Lee," Dr. Thompson replied. "We'll involve stakeholders in the development of our mission and vision statements to ensure that they reflect the aspirations and values of our entire school community. By seeking input and feedback from teachers, students, parents, and community members, we can ensure that our mission and vision statements are inclusive and relevant."

She moved on to the next components: **Goals** and **Objectives**. "Our goals are the broad outcomes we aim to achieve, while our objectives are the specific, measurable targets that support our goals," she explained. "Goals provide the overarching direction for our strategic plan, while objectives provide the actionable steps for achieving those goals."

Dr. Thompson stressed the importance of setting SMART objectives: Specific, Measurable, Achievable, Relevant, and Time-bound. "SMART objectives ensure that our goals are clear, achievable, and aligned with our vision and mission."

She clicked to the next slide, which displayed examples of SMART objectives related to academic achievement, student well-being, and community engagement. "Our objectives should address a range of areas, including academic excellence, student support services, staff development, parent involvement, and community partnerships. By setting SMART objectives in each of these areas, we can ensure that our strategic plan is comprehensive and impactful."

Dr. Thompson concluded with a final slide displaying the words: **Clarity, Alignment, Impact**. "By defining clear goals and objectives that are aligned with our mission and vision, we can ensure that our strategic plan sets Crestwood High School on a path towards success. Together, we will turn our vision into reality and create a brighter future for our school community."

As the faculty members filed out of the auditorium, Dr. Thompson could sense their growing clarity and commitment to crafting a strategic plan that would guide Crestwood High School towards its desired future. By emphasizing the importance of each component in shaping their school's direction and priorities, she had empowered her team to approach the task with focus, intentionality, and collaboration. She knew that with their collective effort and dedication, they would develop a strategic plan that laid the foundation for even greater achievements and impact at Crestwood High School.

Setting SMART Goals for Your School

Understanding the significance of setting SMART goals to drive progress and accountability, Dr. Thompson led the faculty through the process of defining specific, measurable, achievable, relevant, and time-bound goals for Crestwood High School. Gathering them once again in the school auditorium, she emphasized the importance of setting goals that were both ambitious and attainable.

"Good afternoon, everyone," Dr. Thompson began, her voice projecting a sense of purpose. "Today, we're going to focus on setting SMART goals for our school—goals that are clear, actionable, and aligned with our vision and mission."

She clicked to the first slide, which displayed the acronym SMART: **Specific, Measurable, Achievable, Relevant, Time-bound**. "SMART goals provide a framework for setting objectives that are both challenging and realistic. They ensure that our efforts are focused, accountable, and ultimately, successful."

Dr. Thompson started with the first component: **Specific**. "Our goals need to be specific and well-defined," she explained. "They should answer the questions: What do we want to achieve? Who is involved? What resources are required? When and where will it happen? Being specific helps us clarify our intentions and focus our efforts."

She moved on to **Measurable**. "Our goals must be measurable, meaning that we can quantify or assess our progress towards achieving them," Dr. Thompson continued. "Measurable goals allow us to track our performance, identify areas for improvement, and celebrate our successes. They provide a clear benchmark for evaluating our progress."

CHAPTER 3: STRATEGIC PLANNING AND GOAL SETTING

Mrs. Lee raised her hand. "Dr. Thompson, how do we ensure that our goals are both ambitious and achievable?"

"Great question, Mrs. Lee," Dr. Thompson replied. "Our goals should be challenging enough to inspire and motivate us, but also realistic and attainable given our resources and constraints. We'll strike a balance between ambition and feasibility by consulting with stakeholders, conducting thorough analysis, and setting incremental milestones."

She clicked to the next slide, which displayed examples of SMART goals related to academic achievement, student engagement, and staff development. "Our goals should be relevant to our school's mission, vision, and priorities," she explained. "They should address key areas of improvement and align with our strategic objectives. By setting relevant goals, we ensure that our efforts contribute to the overall success of Crestwood High School."

Finally, Dr. Thompson emphasized the importance of **Timebound** goals. "Our goals need to have a clear timeframe for completion," she said. "Setting deadlines helps us maintain focus, prioritize our efforts, and hold ourselves accountable for results. It also provides a sense of urgency and momentum to our initiatives."

She concluded with a final slide displaying the words: **Focus, Accountability, Success**. "By setting SMART goals for Crestwood High School, we can ensure that our efforts are targeted, effective, and ultimately, transformative. Together, we will turn our vision into reality and achieve excellence for our school community."

As the faculty members filed out of the auditorium, Dr. Thompson could sense their growing clarity and determination to set SMART goals that would propel Crestwood High School towards its desired future. By emphasizing the importance of specificity, measurability, achievability, relevance, and timeliness in goal-setting, she had equipped her team with a powerful tool for driving progress and accountability. She knew that with their collective effort and commitment, they would achieve remarkable results and make a lasting impact at Crestwood High School.

Engaging Staff and Community in the Planning Process

Recognizing the importance of collaboration and inclusivity in the strategic planning process, Dr. Thompson led the faculty through the vital step of engaging staff and the community in defining Crestwood High School's future direction. Gathering them once again in the school auditorium, she emphasized the significance of diverse perspectives and collective input in shaping their strategic plan.

"Welcome back, everyone," Dr. Thompson began, her voice radiating warmth and inclusivity. "Today, we're going to explore the crucial step of engaging our staff and community in the planning process. Their insights and perspectives are invaluable in ensuring that our strategic plan reflects the needs and aspirations of our entire school community."

She clicked to the first slide, which displayed a diverse group of people—teachers, students, parents, alumni, and community members—engaged in discussion. "Our strategic plan is not just about us—it's about our entire school community," she explained. "By involving staff, students, parents, and community members in the planning process, we ensure that our strategic plan is inclusive, representative, and responsive to their needs."

Dr. Thompson emphasized the importance of creating opportunities for meaningful participation and dialogue. "We'll use a variety of methods to engage stakeholders, including surveys, focus groups, town hall meetings, workshops, and online platforms," she continued. "By providing multiple channels for input, we can reach a diverse range of voices and perspectives."

She moved on to the next step: **Listening**. "Engagement is not just about talking—it's about listening," Dr. Thompson emphasized. "We'll actively listen to the concerns, ideas, and aspirations of our stakeholders, ensuring that their voices are heard and valued. By listening with empathy and openness, we can build trust and rapport with our school community."

Mrs. Lee raised her hand. "Dr. Thompson, how do we ensure that our stakeholders feel genuinely heard and included in the planning process?"

"Excellent question, Mrs. Lee," Dr. Thompson replied. "We'll create a culture of openness and transparency, where everyone feels comfortable sharing their thoughts and ideas. We'll provide regular updates on the planning process, solicit feedback at every stage, and communicate our appreciation for their input."

She clicked to the next slide, which displayed examples of successful engagement strategies, such as community forums, staff retreats, and student-led workshops. "Our engagement efforts will be inclusive and participatory, ensuring that everyone has a seat at the table and a voice in shaping our school's future."

Finally, Dr. Thompson emphasized the importance of **Collaboration**. "By engaging staff and the community in the planning process, we can harness the collective wisdom and creativity of our school community," she concluded. "Together, we will co-create a strategic plan that reflects our shared values, aspirations, and priorities."

As the faculty members filed out of the auditorium, Dr. Thompson could sense their growing excitement and commitment to engaging staff and the community in the planning process. By emphasizing the importance of inclusivity, listening, and collaboration, she had empowered her team to harness the collective power of their school community in shaping Crestwood High School's future direction. She knew that with their collective effort and input, they would develop a strategic plan that truly reflected the needs and aspirations of their diverse stakeholders, setting the stage for even greater success and impact in the years to come.

Monitoring and Evaluating Progress

Understanding that effective monitoring and evaluation are essential for tracking progress and ensuring accountability, Dr. Thompson guided the faculty through the critical step of monitoring and evaluating their strategic plan. Gathering them once again in the school auditorium, she emphasized the importance of ongoing assessment and feedback in driving continuous improvement.

"Good afternoon, everyone," Dr. Thompson began, her voice projecting a sense of purpose. "Today, we're going to focus on monitoring and evaluating the progress of our strategic plan. Monitoring and evaluation are not just about checking boxes—they're about ensuring that our efforts are making a meaningful impact on our school community."

She clicked to the first slide, which displayed a cycle of

monitoring, evaluation, and adjustment. "Monitoring and evaluation provide us with valuable feedback on the effectiveness of our strategic plan," she explained. "They allow us to assess our progress, identify areas for improvement, and make informed decisions about our future direction."

Dr. Thompson started with the first component: **Monitoring**. "Monitoring involves regularly tracking our progress towards achieving our goals and objectives," she continued. "We'll collect data, analyze trends, and measure outcomes to gauge the success of our initiatives. This ongoing monitoring process ensures that we stay on track and can make timely adjustments as needed."

She moved on to **Evaluation**. "Evaluation involves assessing the impact and effectiveness of our strategic plan," Dr. Thompson explained. "We'll use both quantitative and qualitative methods to evaluate our progress, including surveys, focus groups, interviews, and performance metrics. By soliciting feedback from stakeholders, we can gain valuable insights into what's working well and what needs improvement."

Mrs. Lee raised her hand. "Dr. Thompson, how do we ensure that our monitoring and evaluation efforts are thorough and meaningful?"

"Great question, Mrs. Lee," Dr. Thompson replied. "Thorough monitoring and evaluation require clear objectives, reliable data, and systematic analysis. We'll establish key performance indicators (KPIs) for each goal and objective, develop data collection protocols, and designate responsibility for monitoring and evaluation tasks. By following a structured approach, we can ensure that our monitoring and evaluation efforts are comprehensive and actionable."

She clicked to the next slide, which displayed examples of

monitoring and evaluation tools, such as progress trackers, survey instruments, and performance dashboards. "Our monitoring and evaluation efforts will be ongoing and iterative, allowing us to adapt our strategies in real-time based on feedback and evidence."

Finally, Dr. Thompson emphasized the importance of **Adjustment**. "By monitoring and evaluating our progress, we can identify areas for improvement and make timely adjustments to our strategies," she concluded. "This continuous cycle of reflection, assessment, and adjustment ensures that our strategic plan remains relevant, effective, and responsive to the evolving needs of our school community."

As the faculty members filed out of the auditorium, Dr. Thompson could sense their growing appreciation for the importance of monitoring and evaluating progress in driving continuous improvement. By emphasizing the need for thoroughness, accountability, and adaptability in their monitoring and evaluation efforts, she had empowered her team to assess their progress with clarity and purpose. She knew that with their collective commitment and diligence, they would ensure that Crestwood High School's strategic plan remained a dynamic and effective roadmap for achieving their vision and goals.

Adjusting Plans Based on Feedback and Data

Understanding the importance of flexibility and responsiveness in the strategic planning process, Dr. Thompson led the faculty through the crucial step of adjusting plans based on feedback and data. Gathering them once again in the school auditorium, she emphasized the significance of continuous improvement and adaptation in achieving their school's vision and goals.

"Good afternoon, everyone," Dr. Thompson began, her voice resonating with determination. "Today, we're going to explore the critical step of adjusting our plans based on feedback and data. In our journey towards excellence, it's essential that we remain flexible and responsive to changing circumstances and evolving needs."

She clicked to the first slide, which displayed a loop symbolizing the iterative nature of the adjustment process. "Adjusting our plans is not a sign of failure—it's a sign of learning and growth," she explained. "By gathering feedback and analyzing data, we can identify areas for improvement and make informed decisions about how to refine our strategies."

Dr. Thompson started with the importance of **Feedback**. "Feedback provides us with valuable insights into the effectiveness of our initiatives," she continued. "We'll solicit feedback from stakeholders, including teachers, students, parents, and community members, through surveys, focus groups, and interviews. By listening to their perspectives and experiences, we can gain a deeper understanding of what's working well and what needs adjustment."

She moved on to the role of **Data**. "Data allows us to objectively assess our progress and performance," Dr. Thompson explained. "We'll collect and analyze quantitative data, such as academic achievement scores, attendance rates, and disciplinary incidents, as well as qualitative data, such as student testimonials and parent feedback. By triangulating multiple sources of data, we can paint a comprehensive picture of our school's strengths and areas for improvement."

Mr. Harris raised his hand. "Dr. Thompson, how do

we ensure that we're making informed decisions based on feedback and data?"

"Great question, Mr. Harris," Dr. Thompson replied. "Making informed decisions requires careful analysis and deliberation. We'll establish a data-driven decision-making process, where we review feedback and data systematically, identify patterns and trends, and prioritize areas for action. By involving stakeholders in the decision-making process, we can ensure that our adjustments are grounded in evidence and aligned with our school's priorities."

She clicked to the next slide, which displayed examples of adjustments based on feedback and data, such as revising action plans, reallocating resources, and refining strategies. "Our adjustments will be targeted, evidence-based, and purposeful, ensuring that they address the root causes of any challenges or opportunities identified."

Finally, Dr. Thompson emphasized the importance of **Reflection**. "By adjusting our plans based on feedback and data, we demonstrate our commitment to continuous improvement," she concluded. "This ongoing cycle of reflection, feedback, and adjustment ensures that our strategic plan remains dynamic, relevant, and effective in guiding Crestwood High School towards its desired future."

As the faculty members filed out of the auditorium, Dr. Thompson could sense their growing appreciation for the importance of adjusting plans based on feedback and data in driving continuous improvement. By emphasizing the need for flexibility, responsiveness, and evidence-based decision-making, she had empowered her team to approach their strategic planning process with agility and purpose. She knew that with their collective commitment and adaptability, they would ensure that Crestwood High School remained at the forefront of educational excellence, continuously evolving and innovating to meet the needs of their students and community.

4

Chapter 4: Building and Leading Effective Teams

Characteristics of Effective Educational Teams

In the next phase of their leadership journey, Dr. Thompson led the faculty through the exploration of the characteristics that define effective educational teams. Gathering them once again in the school auditorium, she emphasized the importance of cohesion, collaboration, and shared purpose in fostering high-performing teams.

"Good morning, everyone," Dr. Thompson began, her voice filled with energy and anticipation. "Today, we're going to dive into the characteristics of effective educational teams. As leaders in education, our ability to build and lead effective teams is essential for achieving our school's mission and vision."

She clicked to the first slide, which displayed a group of individuals working together towards a common goal. "Effective teams are more than just a collection of individuals—they are cohesive units with a shared sense of purpose and direction," she explained. "They leverage the diverse talents, perspectives, and expertise of their members to achieve common goals and drive positive change."

Dr. Thompson started with the importance of **Trust**. "Trust is the foundation of effective teamwork," she continued. "Members of high-performing teams trust each other's intentions, capabilities, and commitment to the team's success. They communicate openly, support each other, and hold themselves accountable for their actions."

She moved on to **Communication**. "Communication is essential for effective teamwork," Dr. Thompson emphasized. "Teams that communicate openly and transparently are better equipped to share information, resolve conflicts, and make informed decisions. They listen actively, express their ideas clearly, and seek feedback from each other."

Mr. Harris raised his hand. "Dr. Thompson, how do we foster effective communication within our teams?"

"Great question, Mr. Harris," Dr. Thompson replied. "Fostering effective communication requires creating a supportive and inclusive team environment. We'll encourage open dialogue, active listening, and constructive feedback. We'll also provide training and resources to help team members develop their communication skills and overcome any barriers to effective communication."

She clicked to the next slide, which displayed examples of effective communication strategies, such as regular team meetings, brainstorming sessions, and collaborative projects. "Our communication efforts will be proactive and intentional, ensuring that everyone feels valued and heard within the team."

Finally, Dr. Thompson emphasized the importance of **Shared Goals**. "Effective teams have a clear understanding of their goals and objectives," she concluded. "They align their individual efforts with the team's overarching goals, ensuring that everyone is working towards a common purpose. By fostering a shared sense of ownership and accountability, we can empower our teams to achieve remarkable results."

As the faculty members filed out of the auditorium, Dr. Thompson could sense their growing enthusiasm and commitment to building and leading effective teams. By emphasizing the importance of trust, communication, and shared goals in fostering high-performing teams, she had empowered her team to collaborate effectively and achieve their shared vision for Crestwood High School. She knew that with their collective effort and dedication, they would create a supportive and inclusive team culture that propelled their school towards even greater success and impact.

Selecting and Developing Team Members

Understanding the critical role of selecting and developing team members, Dr. Thompson guided the faculty through the process of assembling and nurturing high-performing teams. Gathering them once again in the school auditorium, she emphasized the importance of strategic recruitment, intentional development, and ongoing support in maximizing team effectiveness.

"Welcome back, everyone," Dr. Thompson began, her voice projecting confidence and purpose. "Today, we're going to explore the crucial step of selecting and developing team members. The success of our teams depends on the individuals who comprise them, so it's essential that we invest time and effort in assembling and nurturing high-performing teams."

She clicked to the first slide, which displayed a diverse group of individuals representing various roles and expertise. "Selecting the right team members is key to building effective teams," she explained. "We'll identify individuals who possess the skills, knowledge, and qualities needed to contribute to our team's success. This may include subject matter expertise, leadership abilities, communication skills, and a commitment to our school's mission and values."

Dr. Thompson started with the importance of **Recruitment**. "Recruitment involves identifying and attracting talented individuals to join our teams," she continued. "We'll use a strategic approach to recruitment, leveraging networks, referrals, and targeted outreach efforts to identify candidates who align with our team's needs and priorities. By casting a wide net and seeking diverse perspectives, we can ensure that our teams are inclusive and representative of our school community."

She moved on to **Development**. "Once we've assembled our teams, our focus shifts to developing their skills and capabilities," Dr. Thompson emphasized. "We'll provide training, mentorship, and professional development opportunities to help team members grow and excel in their roles. By investing in their growth and development, we empower our teams to reach their full potential and achieve outstanding results."

Mrs. Lee raised her hand. "Dr. Thompson, how do we ensure that team members have the support they need to succeed?"

"Great question, Mrs. Lee," Dr. Thompson replied. "Supporting team members requires creating a culture of collaboration, recognition, and empowerment. We'll provide ongoing feedback, coaching, and recognition to acknowledge their contributions and address any challenges they may encounter. By fostering a supportive team environment, we can ensure that everyone feels valued and motivated to perform at their best."

She clicked to the next slide, which displayed examples of development opportunities, such as workshops, seminars, coaching sessions, and peer mentoring programs. "Our development efforts will be tailored to the unique needs and aspirations of our team members, ensuring that they have the resources and support they need to succeed."

Finally, Dr. Thompson emphasized the importance of **Retention**. "By selecting and developing our team members effectively, we can enhance retention and loyalty within our teams," she concluded. "High-performing teams are built on a foundation of trust, collaboration, and shared purpose. By investing in our team members' growth and well-being, we create a culture where everyone feels valued and motivated to contribute to our school's success."

As the faculty members filed out of the auditorium, Dr. Thompson could sense their growing appreciation for the importance of selecting and developing team members in building effective teams. By emphasizing the need for strategic recruitment, intentional development, and ongoing support, she had empowered her team to assemble and nurture high-performing teams that would drive positive change and innovation at Crestwood High School. She knew that with their collective effort and dedication, they would create a culture of excellence and collaboration that propelled their school towards even greater heights of achievement and impact.

Fostering Collaboration and Communication

Recognizing the pivotal role of collaboration and communication in team effectiveness, Dr. Thompson guided the faculty through the process of fostering a culture of collaboration and open communication within their teams. Gathering them once again in the school auditorium, she emphasized the importance of trust, transparency, and active engagement in driving successful collaboration.

"Good afternoon, everyone," Dr. Thompson began, her voice filled with warmth and enthusiasm. "Today, we're going to explore the vital role of fostering collaboration and communication within our teams. Collaboration is at the heart of effective teamwork, and open communication is the key to unlocking its full potential."

She clicked to the first slide, which displayed a group of individuals engaged in lively discussion and brainstorming. "Collaboration is more than just working together—it's about leveraging the diverse talents, perspectives, and expertise of our team members to achieve common goals," she explained. "We'll create opportunities for teamwork, encourage knowledge sharing, and celebrate collective achievements. By fostering a collaborative culture, we can harness the collective intelligence and creativity of our teams."

Dr. Thompson started with the importance of **Trust**. "Trust is the foundation of effective collaboration," she continued. "Teams that trust each other's intentions and capabilities are better equipped to work together towards shared goals. We'll build trust within our teams through open communication, mutual respect, and accountability. By fostering a culture of trust, we create a safe and supportive environment where team members feel empowered to take risks and innovate."

She moved on to **Transparency**. "Transparency is essential for fostering collaboration and alignment," Dr. Thompson emphasized. "We'll share information openly, communicate expectations clearly, and involve team members in decision-making processes. By being transparent about our goals, priorities, and challenges, we ensure that everyone is working towards a common purpose and understands their role in achieving it."

Mr. Harris raised his hand. "Dr. Thompson, how do we encourage active participation and engagement within our teams?"

"Great question, Mr. Harris," Dr. Thompson replied. "Encouraging active participation requires creating a supportive and inclusive team environment. We'll provide opportunities for all team members to contribute their ideas, share their expertise, and provide feedback. By valuing and respecting each other's contributions, we foster a sense of ownership and belonging within our teams."

She clicked to the next slide, which displayed examples of collaboration tools and techniques, such as brainstorming sessions, team-building activities, and project management software. "Our collaboration efforts will be purposeful and intentional, ensuring that everyone has the opportunity to contribute their unique talents and perspectives to our team's success."

Finally, Dr. Thompson emphasized the importance of **Feedback**. "Feedback is essential for continuous improvement and growth," she concluded. "We'll provide regular feedback to team members, recognizing their contributions and addressing any areas for improvement. By fostering a culture of feedback, we create a dynamic and responsive team environment where everyone is committed to learning and development."

As the faculty members filed out of the auditorium, Dr. Thompson could sense their growing enthusiasm and commitment to fostering collaboration and communication within their teams. By emphasizing the importance of trust, transparency, and active engagement, she had empowered her team to work together effectively towards their shared goals. She knew that with their collective effort and dedication, they would build a culture of collaboration and communication that drove innovation and excellence at Crestwood High School, ultimately benefiting their students and community.

Conflict Resolution and Consensus Building

Understanding that conflicts are inevitable in any team setting, Dr. Thompson led the faculty through the essential skills of conflict resolution and consensus building. Gathering them once again in the school auditorium, she emphasized the importance of addressing conflicts constructively and fostering consensus to maintain team cohesion and effectiveness.

"Welcome back, everyone," Dr. Thompson began, her voice projecting calm and assurance. "Today, we're going to explore the crucial skills of conflict resolution and consensus building. Conflict is a natural part of teamwork, and how we manage it can either strengthen or weaken our teams."

She clicked to the first slide, which displayed a group of individuals engaged in a discussion with conflicting opinions. "Conflict resolution involves addressing disagreements and tensions in a constructive and collaborative manner," she explained. "We'll develop strategies for managing conflicts effectively, resolving differences, and restoring trust and harmony within our teams."

Dr. Thompson started with the importance of **Understanding**. "Understanding the root causes of conflicts is the first step towards resolving them," she continued. "We'll encourage open dialogue and active listening to uncover the underlying concerns and perspectives of all parties involved. By seeking to understand each other's viewpoints, we can find common ground and work towards mutually acceptable solutions."

She moved on to **Communication**. "Effective communication is essential for resolving conflicts," Dr. Thompson emphasized. "We'll encourage open and honest communication, where team members feel safe to express their concerns and opinions. We'll also teach active listening skills and constructive feedback techniques to facilitate productive discussions and foster empathy and understanding."

Mrs. Lee raised her hand. "Dr. Thompson, how do we ensure that conflicts are resolved in a fair and equitable manner?"

"Great question, Mrs. Lee," Dr. Thompson replied. "Resolving conflicts fairly requires impartiality, respect, and a commitment to finding win-win solutions. We'll establish clear guidelines and processes for resolving conflicts, ensuring that everyone has the opportunity to be heard and that decisions are made based on merit and mutual respect."

She clicked to the next slide, which displayed examples of conflict resolution techniques, such as mediation, negotiation, and compromise. "Our conflict resolution efforts will be guided by the principles of fairness, respect, and collaboration, ensuring that conflicts are resolved in a way that strengthens relationships and promotes team cohesion."

Finally, Dr. Thompson emphasized the importance of

Consensus Building. "Consensus building involves reaching agreement and alignment among team members on key decisions and actions," she concluded. "We'll foster a collaborative decision-making process, where everyone has the opportunity to contribute their ideas and concerns. By seeking consensus, we ensure that decisions are well-informed, supported by all team members, and conducive to achieving our shared goals."

As the faculty members filed out of the auditorium, Dr. Thompson could sense their growing confidence and readiness to address conflicts constructively and build consensus within their teams. By emphasizing the importance of understanding, communication, and collaboration in conflict resolution and consensus building, she had equipped her team with the skills and mindset needed to navigate challenges and maintain team cohesion and effectiveness. She knew that with their collective effort and commitment, they would overcome any obstacles and achieve remarkable results together at Crestwood High School.

Role of Professional Development in Team Building

Recognizing the transformative power of continuous learning and growth, Dr. Thompson led the faculty through the pivotal role of professional development in team building. Gathering them once again in the school auditorium, she emphasized the importance of investing in the ongoing learning and development of team members to enhance their skills, knowledge, and effectiveness.

"Good morning, everyone," Dr. Thompson began, her voice infused with enthusiasm and optimism. "Today, we're going to explore the critical role of professional development in team building. As leaders in education, our commitment to continuous learning and growth is essential for building and leading high-performing teams."

She clicked to the first slide, which displayed a group of educators engaged in various learning activities, such as workshops, seminars, and peer coaching sessions. "Professional development is more than just training—it's about investing in our growth and development as educators and leaders," she explained. "We'll provide opportunities for our team members to enhance their skills, deepen their knowledge, and expand their perspectives through a variety of learning experiences."

Dr. Thompson started with the importance of **Skill Development**. "Skill development is essential for building the capabilities and competencies needed to excel in our roles," she continued. "We'll offer workshops, seminars, and training programs to develop specific skills and competencies relevant to our team's goals and objectives. By investing in our skill development, we can enhance our effectiveness and performance as individual team members."

She moved on to **Knowledge Acquisition**. "Knowledge acquisition is vital for staying informed and up-to-date on best practices and emerging trends in education," Dr. Thompson emphasized. "We'll provide access to resources, such as books, articles, and online courses, to help team members expand their knowledge and expertise. By fostering a culture of continuous learning, we can ensure that our team remains at the forefront of educational innovation and excellence."

Mrs. Lee raised her hand. "Dr. Thompson, how do we ensure that professional development opportunities are relevant and meaningful for our team members?"

"Excellent question, Mrs. Lee," Dr. Thompson replied.

"Relevance and meaning in professional development are achieved by aligning learning opportunities with our team's goals, priorities, and individual development needs. We'll conduct needs assessments, solicit feedback from team members, and tailor professional development plans to address specific skill gaps and areas for growth. By providing personalized and targeted learning experiences, we can ensure that professional development is impactful and meaningful for our team."

She clicked to the next slide, which displayed examples of professional development activities, such as conferences, workshops, webinars, and job shadowing opportunities. "Our professional development efforts will be diverse and multi-faceted, offering a range of learning experiences to accommodate different learning styles and preferences."

Finally, Dr. Thompson emphasized the importance of **Leadership Development**. "Leadership development is essential for building a pipeline of future leaders within our team," she concluded. "We'll provide opportunities for aspiring leaders to develop their leadership skills, build their confidence, and prepare for future leadership roles. By investing in leadership development, we can ensure the long-term success and sustainability of our team and our school."

As the faculty members filed out of the auditorium, Dr. Thompson could sense their growing excitement and commitment to professional development as a catalyst for team building and growth. By emphasizing the importance of skill development, knowledge acquisition, and leadership development, she had empowered her team to embark on a journey of continuous learning and improvement. She knew that with their collective effort and dedication to professional development, they would build a culture of excellence and innovation that propelled Crestwood High School towards even greater heights of achievement and impact.

Evaluating Team Performance and Outcomes

Understanding the importance of accountability and continuous improvement, Dr. Thompson led the faculty through the critical step of evaluating team performance and outcomes. Gathering them once again in the school auditorium, she emphasized the need for systematic assessment and reflection to ensure that their teams were achieving their goals and making a positive impact on their school community.

"Welcome back, everyone," Dr. Thompson began, her voice projecting a sense of focus and determination. "Today, we're going to explore the essential task of evaluating team performance and outcomes. As leaders in education, it's crucial that we hold ourselves accountable for the results we achieve and continuously strive for excellence in our work."

She clicked to the first slide, which displayed a graph showing performance metrics and outcomes. "Evaluating team performance involves assessing our progress towards achieving our goals and objectives," she explained. "We'll collect data, analyze trends, and measure outcomes to gauge the effectiveness of our teams' efforts. By conducting regular evaluations, we can identify areas for improvement and make informed decisions about how to enhance our performance."

Dr. Thompson started with the importance of **Goal Alignment**. "Effective evaluation begins with clearly defined goals and objectives," she continued. "We'll ensure that our team's goals are aligned with our school's mission, vision, and strategic priorities. By establishing clear expectations and benchmarks for success, we can measure our progress and outcomes with clarity and purpose."

She moved on to **Performance Metrics**. "Performance metrics provide us with objective data to assess our team's performance," Dr. Thompson emphasized. "We'll establish key performance indicators (KPIs) for each goal and objective, such as student achievement scores, graduation rates, and stakeholder satisfaction surveys. By tracking these metrics over time, we can monitor our progress and identify areas for improvement."

Mr. Harris raised his hand. "Dr. Thompson, how do we ensure that our evaluation processes are fair and equitable?"

"Excellent question, Mr. Harris," Dr. Thompson replied. "Ensuring fairness and equity in evaluation requires transparency, consistency, and inclusivity. We'll establish clear evaluation criteria and processes, communicate expectations openly, and involve team members in the evaluation process. By soliciting feedback and input from all stakeholders, we can ensure that our evaluation processes are fair, objective, and reflective of our team's collective efforts and contributions."

She clicked to the next slide, which displayed examples of evaluation tools and techniques, such as performance assessments, self-assessments, and peer reviews. "Our evaluation efforts will be systematic and comprehensive, allowing us to assess our team's performance from multiple perspectives and identify opportunities for growth and improvement."

Finally, Dr. Thompson emphasized the importance of **Reflection**. "Reflection is essential for learning and growth," she concluded. "We'll encourage our team members to reflect on their performance, celebrate successes, and identify lessons learned from challenges and setbacks. By fostering a culture of reflection, we can cultivate a mindset of continuous improvement and excellence within our teams."

As the faculty members filed out of the auditorium, Dr. Thompson could sense their growing appreciation for the importance of evaluating team performance and outcomes in driving continuous improvement. By emphasizing the need for goal alignment, performance metrics, and reflection, she had empowered her team to assess their progress with clarity and purpose. She knew that with their collective commitment and dedication to evaluation, they would ensure that Crestwood High School's teams remained effective, responsive, and impactful in achieving their shared vision and goals.

5

Chapter 5: Instructional Leadership

Role of the Leader in Curriculum Development

In the next phase of their leadership journey, Dr. Thompson guided the faculty through the pivotal role of instructional leadership, starting with the leader's involvement in curriculum development. Gathering them once again in the school auditorium, she emphasized the importance of shaping the educational experience through thoughtful curriculum design and implementation.

"Good morning, everyone," Dr. Thompson began, her voice filled with enthusiasm and purpose. "Today, we're going to delve into the critical role of instructional leadership, starting with the leader's involvement in curriculum development. As leaders in education, it's essential that we play an active role in shaping the curriculum to ensure that it meets the needs of our students and aligns with our school's mission and vision."

She clicked to the first slide, which displayed a blueprint representing the curriculum development process. "Curriculum development is the foundation of effective teaching and learning," she explained. "It involves designing, implementing, and evaluating the educational programs and experiences that our students engage in. As instructional leaders, we have a responsibility to lead this process with vision, expertise, and a commitment to excellence."

Dr. Thompson started with the importance of **Vision**. "Vision is essential for guiding curriculum development," she continued. "We'll articulate a clear vision for teaching and learning that reflects our school's values, priorities, and aspirations. This vision will serve as a guiding framework for curriculum development, ensuring that our educational programs are coherent, cohesive, and aligned with our overarching goals."

She moved on to **Expertise**. "Expertise is essential for ensuring the quality and relevance of our curriculum," Dr. Thompson emphasized. "We'll draw on our knowledge of educational research, best practices, and standards to inform our curriculum decisions. By staying informed about the latest trends and developments in education, we can ensure that our curriculum remains current, rigorous, and responsive to the needs of our students."

Mrs. Lee raised her hand. "Dr. Thompson, how do we ensure that our curriculum reflects the diverse needs and backgrounds of our students?"

"Excellent question, Mrs. Lee," Dr. Thompson replied. "Ensuring diversity and inclusivity in our curriculum requires intentional efforts to incorporate diverse perspectives, experiences, and voices. We'll engage stakeholders, including students, parents, teachers, and community members, in the curriculum development process. By soliciting input and feedback from diverse perspectives, we can ensure that our curriculum reflects the rich diversity of our school community."

She clicked to the next slide, which displayed examples of curriculum development strategies, such as needs assessments, curriculum mapping, and stakeholder engagement. "Our curriculum development efforts will be collaborative, data-driven, and responsive to the evolving needs of our students and community."

Finally, Dr. Thompson emphasized the importance of **Alignment**. "Alignment is essential for ensuring coherence and consistency across our curriculum," she concluded. "We'll align our curriculum with state standards, district goals, and academic benchmarks to ensure that our students receive a rigorous and comprehensive education. By aligning our curriculum with our school's vision and goals, we can ensure that every aspect of our educational program contributes to the success and well-being of our students."

As the faculty members filed out of the auditorium, Dr. Thompson could sense their growing appreciation for the role of instructional leadership in curriculum development. By emphasizing the need for vision, expertise, diversity, and alignment, she had empowered her team to lead with purpose and excellence in shaping the educational experience for their students at Crestwood High School. She knew that with their collective effort and dedication, they would create a curriculum that inspired, challenged, and empowered their students to achieve their full potential and become lifelong learners and leaders.

Promoting Best Teaching Practices

Continuing their exploration of instructional leadership, Dr. Thompson shifted the focus to the crucial task of promoting best teaching practices among the faculty. Gathering them once again in the school auditorium, she emphasized the importance of fostering a culture of excellence and continuous improvement in teaching and learning.

"Good afternoon, everyone," Dr. Thompson began, her voice resonating with passion and dedication. "Today, we're going to dive into the essential role of instructional leaders in promoting best teaching practices. As leaders in education, it's our responsibility to create an environment where excellence in teaching and learning thrives."

She clicked to the first slide, which displayed a collage of effective teaching practices, such as differentiated instruction, formative assessment, and student-centered learning. "Promoting best teaching practices is about empowering our teachers to deliver high-quality instruction that meets the diverse needs of our students and fosters their growth and achievement," she explained.

Dr. Thompson started with the importance of **Modeling**. "Modeling best teaching practices begins with us," she continued. "As instructional leaders, we must lead by example, demonstrating effective teaching strategies, instructional methods, and classroom management techniques. By modeling best practices in our own teaching and leadership, we inspire and motivate our teachers to strive for excellence in their practice."

She moved on to **Support and Professional Development**. "Supporting our teachers' professional growth and development is essential for promoting best teaching practices,"

Dr. Thompson emphasized. "We'll provide opportunities for ongoing training, mentorship, and coaching to help our teachers enhance their instructional skills and strategies. By investing in their professional development, we empower our teachers to continuously improve and innovate in their practice."

Mr. Harris raised his hand. "Dr. Thompson, how do we ensure that best teaching practices are effectively implemented and sustained across our school?"

"Great question, Mr. Harris," Dr. Thompson replied. "Ensuring effective implementation and sustainability requires a systematic approach to professional learning and collaboration. We'll establish professional learning communities (PLCs) where teachers can collaborate, share best practices, and support each other in implementing new instructional strategies. By creating a culture of collaboration and continuous improvement, we can ensure that best teaching practices become ingrained in our school's culture and ethos."

She clicked to the next slide, which displayed examples of professional development opportunities, such as workshops, peer observations, and action research projects. "Our professional development efforts will be tailored to the unique needs and aspirations of our teachers, ensuring that they have the support and resources they need to excel in their practice."

Finally, Dr. Thompson emphasized the importance of **Feedback and Reflection**. "Feedback and reflection are essential for promoting continuous improvement in teaching and learning," she concluded. "We'll provide regular feedback to our teachers, acknowledging their strengths and providing constructive guidance for growth. We'll also encourage them to reflect on their practice, identify areas for improvement, and set goals for professional growth. By fostering a culture of feedback and reflection, we can ensure that our teachers are constantly striving to enhance their practice and meet the evolving needs of our students."

As the faculty members filed out of the auditorium, Dr. Thompson could sense their growing commitment and enthusiasm for promoting best teaching practices. By emphasizing the importance of modeling, support and professional development, collaboration, and feedback and reflection, she had empowered her team to cultivate a culture of excellence and continuous improvement in teaching and learning at Crestwood High School. She knew that with their collective effort and dedication, they would inspire and empower their students to achieve their full potential and become lifelong learners and leaders.

Supporting Teacher Professional Growth

Dr. Thompson continued her discourse on instructional leadership, delving into the pivotal role of supporting teacher professional growth. Gathering the faculty once more in the school auditorium, she emphasized the importance of fostering a culture of continuous learning and development among educators.

"Good morning, everyone," Dr. Thompson greeted, her voice infused with warmth and encouragement. "Today, we're going to explore the crucial task of supporting teacher professional growth. As instructional leaders, it's imperative that we invest in the growth and development of our teachers to ensure they have the tools and skills needed to excel in their practice."

She clicked to the first slide, depicting a pathway symbolizing the journey of professional growth. "Supporting teacher professional growth is about providing the guidance, resources, and opportunities for our teachers to expand their knowledge, skills, and effectiveness as educators," she explained.

Dr. Thompson began with the importance of **Individualized Support**. "Each teacher has unique strengths, challenges, and professional goals," she continued. "We'll provide individualized support to help teachers identify their areas for growth, set meaningful goals, and develop personalized professional learning plans. By tailoring our support to meet the specific needs of each teacher, we can ensure that they receive the targeted guidance and resources they need to succeed."

She moved on to **Coaching and Mentoring**. "Coaching and mentoring are powerful tools for supporting teacher professional growth," Dr. Thompson emphasized. "We'll pair teachers with experienced mentors or instructional coaches who can provide guidance, feedback, and support as they work to improve their practice. By fostering a culture of coaching and mentoring, we create a collaborative and supportive environment where teachers can learn from each other and grow together."

Mrs. Lee raised her hand. "Dr. Thompson, how do we ensure that our support is effective in promoting teacher growth?"

"An excellent question, Mrs. Lee," Dr. Thompson replied. "Ensuring the effectiveness of our support requires ongoing communication, feedback, and reflection. We'll regularly check in with teachers to assess their progress, solicit feedback on their support needs, and adjust our approach as needed. By fostering open dialogue and collaboration, we can ensure that our support efforts are responsive to the evolving needs of our teachers and promote meaningful growth and development."

She clicked to the next slide, displaying examples of coaching sessions, professional learning communities, and peer observations. "Our support for teacher professional growth will be comprehensive and multifaceted, offering a range of opportunities for learning, collaboration, and reflection."

Finally, Dr. Thompson emphasized the importance of **Celebrating Success**. "Celebrating successes, big and small, is essential for fostering a culture of continuous improvement and growth," she concluded. "We'll recognize and celebrate the achievements of our teachers, whether it's mastering a new teaching strategy, achieving a professional milestone, or making a positive impact on student learning. By celebrating successes, we inspire and motivate our teachers to continue their journey of professional growth and excellence."

As the faculty members filed out of the auditorium, Dr. Thompson could sense their renewed dedication and enthusiasm for supporting teacher professional growth. By emphasizing the importance of individualized support, coaching and mentoring, ongoing communication, and celebrating success, she had empowered her team to foster a culture of continuous learning and development at Crestwood High School. She knew that with their collective effort and commitment, they would create an environment where every teacher had the opportunity to thrive and excel in their practice, ultimately benefiting their students and school community.

Implementing Effective Assessment Strategies

Continuing her discourse on instructional leadership, Dr. Thompson delved into the critical role of implementing effective assessment strategies to support student learning. Gathering the faculty once more in the school auditorium, she emphasized the importance of using assessments as tools for understanding student progress and informing instruction.

"Welcome back, everyone," Dr. Thompson greeted, her voice filled with enthusiasm and determination. "Today, we're going to explore the vital task of implementing effective assessment strategies. As instructional leaders, it's essential that we use assessments to gain insights into our students' learning and guide our instructional decisions."

She clicked to the first slide, displaying various assessment tools and methods. "Effective assessment strategies allow us to gauge student understanding, monitor progress, and identify areas for growth," she explained. "By using a variety of assessment techniques, we can gather comprehensive data on student learning and tailor our instruction to meet their individual needs."

Dr. Thompson began with the importance of **Formative Assessment**. "Formative assessment provides timely feedback to students and teachers during the learning process," she continued. "We'll incorporate formative assessment strategies, such as quizzes, exit tickets, and classroom discussions, to monitor student progress and adjust our instruction accordingly. By using formative assessment, we can identify misconceptions, address learning gaps, and ensure that all students are on track to meet their learning goals."

She moved on to **Summative Assessment**. "Summative assessment measures student achievement at the end of a unit, course, or school year," Dr. Thompson emphasized. "We'll administer summative assessments, such as tests, projects, and portfolios, to evaluate student learning outcomes and determine their mastery of content and skills. By using summative assessment, we can assess the effectiveness of our instruction and make data-driven decisions to improve student learning."

Mr. Harris raised his hand. "Dr. Thompson, how do we ensure that our assessments are fair and equitable for all students?"

"An excellent question, Mr. Harris," Dr. Thompson replied. "Ensuring fairness and equity in assessments requires careful attention to assessment design, administration, and interpretation. We'll use a variety of assessment techniques and formats to accommodate diverse learning styles and preferences. We'll also provide accommodations and modifications for students with special needs or English language learners to ensure that assessments accurately measure their learning. By adhering to best practices in assessment, we can ensure that all students have the opportunity to demonstrate their knowledge and skills effectively."

She clicked to the next slide, which displayed examples of assessment tools and rubrics. "Our assessment strategies will be comprehensive and inclusive, allowing us to gather accurate and meaningful data on student learning."

Finally, Dr. Thompson emphasized the importance of **Data Analysis**. "Data analysis is essential for interpreting assessment results and informing instructional decisions," she concluded. "We'll analyze assessment data to identify trends, patterns, and areas for improvement in student learning. By using data to guide our instruction, we can ensure that our teaching is responsive to the needs of our students and supports their growth and achievement."

As the faculty members filed out of the auditorium, Dr. Thompson could sense their growing appreciation for the importance of implementing effective assessment strategies. By emphasizing the need for formative and summative assessment, fairness and equity, and data analysis, she had equipped her team with the tools and knowledge needed to support student learning and success at Crestwood High School. She knew that with their collective effort and commitment to effective assessment, they would ensure that every student received a high-quality education that prepared them for success in college, career, and life.

Using Data to Drive Instructional Decisions

Dr. Thompson proceeded with her discussion on instructional leadership, focusing on the transformative role of using data to inform instructional decisions. Assembled once again in the school auditorium, the faculty listened intently as she underscored the importance of leveraging data to personalize instruction and support student learning.

"Good afternoon, everyone," Dr. Thompson greeted, her tone projecting a sense of purpose and determination. "Today, we're going to delve into the critical task of using data to drive instructional decisions. As instructional leaders, it's essential that we harness the power of data to understand student needs, identify areas for improvement, and optimize teaching and learning."

She clicked to the first slide, displaying graphs and charts representing various types of educational data. "Data-driven decision-making allows us to make informed choices about instruction, curriculum, and support services," she explained. "By analyzing data on student performance, engagement, and growth, we can tailor our instructional strategies to meet the unique needs of each student and maximize their learning outcomes."

Dr. Thompson began with the importance of **Assessment Data**. "Assessment data provides valuable insights into student learning and progress," she continued. "We'll analyze assessment results to identify strengths, weaknesses, and areas for growth in student performance. By using assessment data, we can differentiate instruction, provide targeted interventions, and scaffold learning experiences to meet the diverse needs of our students."

She moved on to **Attendance and Engagement Data**. "Attendance and engagement data offer insights into students' level of participation and involvement in learning activities," Dr. Thompson emphasized. "We'll monitor attendance rates, participation levels, and engagement indicators to identify students who may be at risk of falling behind or disengaging from school. By using attendance and engagement data, we can intervene early, provide additional support, and re-engage students in their learning."

Mrs. Lee raised her hand. "Dr. Thompson, how do we ensure that our data analysis leads to actionable insights and meaningful change in instruction?"

"An excellent question, Mrs. Lee," Dr. Thompson replied. "Ensuring that our data analysis leads to actionable insights requires a systematic approach to data interpretation, collaboration, and reflection. We'll analyze data collaboratively with our instructional teams, identify trends and patterns, and brainstorm potential instructional strategies and interventions. By engaging in ongoing reflection and dialogue, we can translate data into action and continuously improve our instructional practices."

She clicked to the next slide, which displayed examples of data dashboards, trend analyses, and collaborative data meetings. "Our data-driven decision-making process will be transparent, collaborative, and focused on student learning outcomes."

Finally, Dr. Thompson emphasized the importance of **Continuous Improvement**. "Continuous improvement is at the heart of data-driven decision-making," she concluded. "We'll use data to identify areas for improvement, implement targeted interventions, and monitor progress towards our goals. By embracing a culture of continuous improvement, we can ensure that every decision we make is guided by evidence and focused on advancing student learning and success."

As the faculty members filed out of the auditorium, Dr. Thompson could sense their growing appreciation for the transformative potential of using data to drive instructional decisions. By emphasizing the importance of assessment data, attendance and engagement data, actionable insights, and continuous improvement, she had empowered her team to harness the power of data to support student learning and achievement at Crestwood High School. She knew that with their collective effort and commitment to data-driven decision-making, they would ensure that every student received a high-quality education that prepared them for success in college, career, and life.

Fostering a Culture of Continuous Improvement

Dr. Thompson transitioned seamlessly into the final subpoint of her discussion on instructional leadership, emphasizing the importance of fostering a culture of continuous improvement among the faculty. Assembled once again in the school auditorium, the faculty listened attentively as she articulated the vision of a school community committed to ongoing growth and excellence.

"Good morning, everyone," Dr. Thompson greeted, her voice resonating with enthusiasm and conviction. "Today, we're going to explore the transformative power of fostering a culture of continuous improvement. As instructional leaders, it's imperative that we cultivate an environment where reflection, collaboration, and innovation thrive."

She clicked to the first slide, displaying images of teamwork, professional development, and goal setting. "A culture of continuous improvement is characterized by a shared commitment to learning, growth, and excellence," she explained. "By embracing a growth mindset and a spirit of inquiry, we can create a community where every member is empowered to learn from their experiences, seek feedback, and strive for excellence in their practice."

Dr. Thompson began with the importance of **Reflection**. "Reflection is the cornerstone of continuous improvement," she continued. "We'll encourage our teachers to reflect on their practice, identify areas for growth, and set goals for improvement. By engaging in regular reflection, we can learn from our experiences, celebrate successes, and identify opportunities for growth."

She moved on to **Collaboration**. "Collaboration is essential for fostering a culture of continuous improvement," Dr. Thompson emphasized. "We'll create opportunities for teachers to collaborate, share best practices, and learn from each other. By working together, we can leverage our collective expertise and creativity to solve problems, innovate in our practice, and achieve our shared goals."

Mrs. Lee raised her hand. "Dr. Thompson, how do we ensure that our efforts towards continuous improvement are sustained over time?"

"An excellent question, Mrs. Lee," Dr. Thompson replied. "Sustaining continuous improvement requires ongoing support, accountability, and celebration of progress. We'll provide support and resources to help teachers achieve their goals, hold ourselves and each other accountable for our commitments, and celebrate our successes along the way. By creating a supportive and affirming environment, we can ensure that our efforts towards continuous improvement are sustained and impactful."

She clicked to the next slide, which displayed examples of collaborative projects, professional learning communities, and recognition programs. "Our efforts towards continuous improvement will be collaborative, intentional, and sustained over time."

Finally, Dr. Thompson emphasized the importance of **Innovation**. "Innovation is the engine of continuous improvement," she concluded. "We'll encourage our teachers to embrace innovation, take risks, and explore new ideas and approaches in their practice. By fostering a culture of innovation, we can push the boundaries of what's possible and create new opportunities for learning and growth."

As the faculty members filed out of the auditorium, Dr. Thompson could sense their renewed commitment to fostering a culture of continuous improvement. By emphasizing the importance of reflection, collaboration, accountability, and innovation, she had empowered her team to embrace a growth mindset and strive for excellence in their practice. She knew that with their collective effort and dedication to continuous improvement, they would create a school community where every member thrived and every student achieved their full potential.

6

Chapter 6: Fostering a Positive School Culture

Defining and Understanding School Culture

Dr. Thompson shifted gears to explore the intricacies of fostering a positive school culture, starting with the foundational step of defining and understanding what school culture truly encompasses. Assembled once more in the school auditorium, the faculty leaned forward attentively, eager to delve into this crucial aspect of their leadership journey.

"Good afternoon, everyone," Dr. Thompson greeted warmly, her presence commanding the attention of the room. "Today, we embark on a journey to explore the essence of school culture and how it shapes our daily interactions, practices, and ultimately, the learning experiences of our students."

She clicked to the first slide, which displayed images representing diverse aspects of school life, from student clubs to staff collaboration. "School culture is the heartbeat of our educational community," she began. "It encompasses the beliefs, values, norms, and traditions that define who we are as a school and how we interact with one another."

Dr. Thompson emphasized the importance of **Beliefs and Values**. "Beliefs and values form the foundation of our school culture," she continued. "They shape our attitudes, priorities, and decisions, influencing everything from how we approach teaching and learning to how we resolve conflicts and celebrate successes. By understanding and articulating our shared beliefs and values, we can create a cohesive and unified school culture that fosters a sense of belonging and purpose among all members of our community."

She moved on to **Norms and Expectations**. "Norms and expectations are the unwritten rules and standards that govern behavior within our school," Dr. Thompson explained. "They define what is considered acceptable and appropriate conduct and shape the social dynamics and interactions within our community. By establishing clear norms and expectations, we can create a positive and supportive school environment where everyone feels respected, valued, and safe."

Mr. Harris raised his hand. "Dr. Thompson, how do we ensure that our school culture reflects the diverse perspectives and experiences of our students and staff?"

"An excellent question, Mr. Harris," Dr. Thompson replied. "Ensuring inclusivity and diversity in our school culture requires intentional efforts to listen, learn, and celebrate the unique identities and backgrounds of all members of our community. We'll engage in dialogue, solicit feedback, and incorporate diverse voices and perspectives into our decision-making processes. By fostering a culture of inclusivity and belonging, we can create an environment where everyone feels respected, valued, and empowered to thrive."

She clicked to the next slide, which displayed examples of school rituals, traditions, and symbols. "Our school culture is shaped by the rituals, traditions, and symbols that define our shared identity and sense of community," she continued. "From morning assemblies to graduation ceremonies, from school mascots to alma mater songs, these rituals and traditions bind us together and create a sense of continuity and belonging across generations of students and staff."

Finally, Dr. Thompson emphasized the importance of **Continuous Reflection and Improvement**. "Fostering a positive school culture is an ongoing process," she concluded. "We'll engage in continuous reflection, dialogue, and collaboration to assess our current culture, identify areas for improvement, and implement strategies to strengthen and enhance our school culture over time. By committing to continuous reflection and improvement, we can ensure that our school culture remains vibrant, inclusive, and supportive of the needs and aspirations of all members of our community."

As the faculty members filed out of the auditorium, Dr. Thompson could sense their renewed appreciation for the complexity and significance of school culture. By emphasizing the importance of beliefs and values, norms and expectations, inclusivity and diversity, rituals and traditions, and continuous reflection and improvement, she had laid the groundwork for their collective journey towards fostering a positive and inclusive school culture at Crestwood High School. She knew that with their commitment and dedication, they would create a school community where every member felt valued, supported, and empowered to thrive.

Strategies for Building a Positive Culture

Dr. Thompson continued her exploration of fostering a positive school culture, transitioning seamlessly into discussing practical strategies for nurturing an environment where students and staff flourish. Assembled once more in the school auditorium, the faculty listened intently, eager to glean insights into cultivating a vibrant and supportive school culture.

"Good morning, everyone," Dr. Thompson greeted, her voice brimming with energy and anticipation. "Today, we're diving into the heart of building a positive school culture by exploring actionable strategies that empower us to create an environment where every member feels valued, respected, and empowered."

She clicked to the first slide, which displayed a roadmap symbolizing the journey towards a positive school culture. "Building a positive culture requires intentional efforts and collective commitment," she began. "It's about fostering a sense of belonging, promoting positive relationships, and creating opportunities for growth and development."

Dr. Thompson emphasized the importance of **Relationship Building**. "Relationships are the foundation of a positive school culture," she continued. "We'll prioritize building strong, trusting relationships among students, staff, families, and community members. By fostering open communication, empathy, and mutual respect, we can create a supportive and inclusive school community where everyone feels valued and connected."

She moved on to **Celebrating Diversity and Inclusion**. "Diversity and inclusion enrich our school community and enhance our learning experiences," Dr. Thompson emphasized. "We'll celebrate the unique identities, backgrounds, and perspectives of all members of our community. By embracing diversity and promoting inclusivity, we can create a culture where everyone feels welcome, respected, and empowered to be their authentic selves."

Mrs. Lee raised her hand. "Dr. Thompson, how do we ensure that our efforts to build a positive culture are sustained over time?"

"An excellent question, Mrs. Lee," Dr. Thompson replied. "Sustaining a positive culture requires ongoing nurturing, reinforcement, and adaptation. We'll embed our values and principles into every aspect of school life, from our policies and practices to our rituals and traditions. By fostering a culture of shared ownership and accountability, we can ensure that our efforts to build a positive culture are sustained and ingrained in the fabric of our school community."

She clicked to the next slide, which displayed examples of community-building activities, cultural celebrations, and inclusive practices. "Our strategies for building a positive culture will be diverse, dynamic, and responsive to the evolving needs and aspirations of our school community."

Finally, Dr. Thompson emphasized the importance of **Continuous Feedback and Improvement**. "Continuous feedback and improvement are essential for strengthening our culture and addressing areas for growth," she concluded. "We'll solicit feedback from students, staff, families, and community members, and use it to inform our decisions and actions. By committing to continuous reflection and improvement, we can ensure that our school culture remains vibrant, inclusive, and supportive for all."

As the faculty members filed out of the auditorium, Dr. Thompson could sense their renewed enthusiasm and determination to build a positive school culture. By emphasizing the importance of relationship building, celebrating diversity and inclusion, sustainability, and continuous feedback and improvement, she had equipped her team with the tools and strategies needed to foster a thriving and inclusive school community at Crestwood High School. She knew that with their collective effort and commitment, they would create a culture where every member felt valued, supported, and empowered to thrive.

Role of Leadership in Shaping Culture

Dr. Thompson transitioned seamlessly into the next subpoint of her discussion on fostering a positive school culture, highlighting the pivotal role of leadership in shaping and nurturing a culture of excellence. Assembled once again in the school auditorium, the faculty leaned forward attentively, eager to explore the ways in which their leadership could influence the cultural landscape of Crestwood High School.

"Good afternoon, everyone," Dr. Thompson greeted, her voice infused with warmth and conviction. "Today, we're going to delve into the transformative power of leadership in shaping and sustaining a positive school culture. As leaders in education, it's imperative that we model the values, behaviors, and attitudes that we seek to cultivate in our school community."

She clicked to the first slide, which displayed images of leadership in action, from team-building exercises to community outreach initiatives. "Leadership sets the tone for our school culture," she began. "It's about inspiring, empowering, and guiding others towards a shared vision of excellence and inclusivity."

Dr. Thompson emphasized the importance of **Visionary Leadership**. "Visionary leadership provides a sense of purpose and direction for our school community," she continued. "We'll articulate a compelling vision that reflects our shared values, aspirations, and priorities. By communicating our vision with clarity and passion, we can inspire others to join us in our journey towards a positive and inclusive school culture."

She moved on to **Leading by Example**. "Leadership is not just about words; it's about actions," Dr. Thompson emphasized. "We'll lead by example, demonstrating integrity, empathy, and accountability in everything we do. By modeling the behaviors and attitudes that we expect from others, we can create a culture of trust, respect, and collaboration."

Mr. Harris raised his hand. "Dr. Thompson, how do we ensure that our leadership is inclusive and responsive to the needs of all members of our school community?"

"An excellent question, Mr. Harris," Dr. Thompson replied. "Ensuring inclusive leadership requires listening, learning, and actively seeking input from diverse perspectives and voices. We'll engage in dialogue, solicit feedback, and incorporate diverse viewpoints into our decision-making processes. By fostering a culture of inclusivity and collaboration, we can ensure that our leadership is responsive to the needs and aspirations of all members of our school community."

She clicked to the next slide, which displayed examples of collaborative leadership, shared decision-making, and servant leadership. "Our leadership approach will be collaborative, inclusive, and focused on serving the needs of our school community."

Finally, Dr. Thompson emphasized the importance of **Empowering Others**. "Empowering others is at the heart of effective leadership," she concluded. "We'll empower teachers, students, families, and community members to take ownership of our school culture and contribute to its growth and development. By fostering a culture of shared leadership and collective responsibility, we can create an environment where everyone feels valued, respected, and empowered to make a difference."

As the faculty members filed out of the auditorium, Dr. Thompson could sense their growing commitment and enthusiasm for their roles as leaders in shaping the culture of Crestwood High School. By emphasizing the importance of visionary leadership, leading by example, inclusivity, and empowering others, she had equipped her team with the knowledge and inspiration needed to lead with purpose and passion. She knew that with their collective effort and dedication, they would create a school community where every member felt valued, supported, and empowered to thrive.

Celebrating Successes and Addressing Challenges

Dr. Thompson seamlessly transitioned into the next subpoint of her discussion on fostering a positive school culture, emphasizing the importance of celebrating successes and addressing challenges as key elements in nurturing a thriving educational community. Assembled once more in the school auditorium, the faculty listened intently, eager to explore the dynamics of acknowledging achievements and overcoming obstacles together.

"Good morning, everyone," Dr. Thompson greeted, her voice radiating warmth and encouragement. "Today, we're going to delve into the vital practice of celebrating successes and addressing challenges as we strive to cultivate a positive and resilient school culture. As leaders, it's essential that we create opportunities to recognize achievements and support one another through difficult times."

She clicked to the first slide, displaying images of celebrations, team huddles, and problem-solving sessions. "Celebrating successes is a cornerstone of a positive school culture," she began. "It's about acknowledging the accomplishments, big and small, that contribute to the growth and success of our school community."

Dr. Thompson emphasized the importance of **Recognition and Appreciation**. "Recognition and appreciation fuel motivation and morale," she continued. "We'll celebrate achievements, milestones, and contributions from students, staff, families, and community members. By shining a spotlight on excellence and showing gratitude for the efforts of others, we can foster a culture of positivity and empowerment."

She moved on to **Reflection and Learning**. "Reflection is essential for growth and improvement," Dr. Thompson emphasized. "We'll take time to reflect on our successes, analyzing what worked well and why. We'll also examine our challenges, identifying opportunities for growth and learning. By engaging in reflective practice, we can extract valuable lessons from our experiences and continuously strive for excellence."

Mrs. Lee raised her hand. "Dr. Thompson, how do we address challenges in a way that fosters resilience and unity?"

"An excellent question, Mrs. Lee," Dr. Thompson replied. "Addressing challenges requires resilience, collaboration, and a shared commitment to overcoming obstacles together. We'll approach challenges as opportunities for growth, rallying together as a school community to brainstorm solutions, provide support, and persevere in the face of adversity. By fostering a culture of resilience and unity, we can navigate challenges with strength and determination, emerging stronger and more connected than before."

She clicked to the next slide, which displayed examples of team celebrations, problem-solving workshops, and resilience-building activities. "Our approach to celebrating successes and addressing challenges will be collaborative, reflective, and focused on building a resilient and supportive school community."

Finally, Dr. Thompson emphasized the importance of **Continuous Improvement**. "Continuous improvement is at the heart of our efforts to foster a positive school culture," she concluded. "We'll learn from our successes and challenges, adapt our strategies, and continuously strive to create a school community where every member feels valued, supported, and empowered to thrive."

As the faculty members filed out of the auditorium, Dr. Thompson could sense their renewed commitment to celebrating successes and addressing challenges as they worked together to foster a positive school culture. By emphasizing the importance of recognition and appreciation, reflection and learning, resilience and unity, and continuous improvement, she had equipped her team with the tools and mindset needed to navigate the ups and downs of their educational journey with grace and resilience. She knew that with their collective effort and dedication, they would create a school community where every member felt valued, supported, and empowered to thrive.

Promoting Equity and Inclusion

Dr. Thompson seamlessly transitioned into the next subpoint of her discussion on fostering a positive school culture, highlighting the paramount importance of promoting equity and inclusion as foundational pillars of their educational community. Assembled once more in the school auditorium, the faculty listened intently, ready to explore the ways in which they could create a school environment where every individual felt valued, respected, and empowered to succeed.

"Good afternoon, everyone," Dr. Thompson greeted warmly, her voice resonating with passion and conviction. "Today, we're embarking on a journey to explore the transformative power of promoting equity and inclusion in shaping our school culture. As leaders, it's imperative that we champion diversity, embrace inclusivity, and dismantle barriers to opportunity."

She clicked to the first slide, which displayed images representing diversity, inclusion, and belonging. "Promoting equity and inclusion is not just a goal; it's a moral imperative," she began. "It's about creating a school environment where every student, regardless of their background, identity, or ability, feels seen, heard, and valued."

Dr. Thompson emphasized the importance of **Equity in Education**. "Equity in education means ensuring that every student has access to the resources, support, and opportunities they need to succeed," she continued. "We'll examine our practices, policies, and systems through an equity lens, identifying and addressing inequities that may exist. By promoting equity, we can create a level playing field where all students have the chance to thrive."

She moved on to **Inclusive Practices**. "Inclusive practices embrace the diversity of our school community and create a sense of belonging for all," Dr. Thompson emphasized. "We'll cultivate an environment where differences are celebrated, perspectives are valued, and every voice is heard. By fostering inclusivity, we can create a culture where everyone feels respected, valued, and empowered to contribute."

Mr. Harris raised his hand. "Dr. Thompson, how do we ensure that our efforts towards equity and inclusion are meaningful and sustainable?"

"An excellent question, Mr. Harris," Dr. Thompson replied. "Ensuring meaningful and sustainable equity and inclusion requires ongoing commitment, collaboration, and accountability. We'll engage in dialogue, solicit feedback, and collaborate with students, staff, families, and community members to co-create solutions that address the unique needs and aspirations of our school community. By embedding equity and inclusion into our culture, policies, and practices, we can create lasting change that benefits everyone."

She clicked to the next slide, which displayed examples of equity audits, inclusive curriculum, and culturally responsive teaching practices. "Our efforts towards promoting equity and inclusion will be intentional, collaborative, and focused on creating a school community where every member feels valued, respected, and empowered to succeed."

Finally, Dr. Thompson emphasized the importance of **Continuous Learning and Growth**. "Promoting equity and inclusion is a journey, not a destination," she concluded. "We'll commit to continuous learning, reflection, and growth, challenging ourselves to confront biases, dismantle barriers, and create a more just and equitable school community for all."

As the faculty members filed out of the auditorium, Dr.

Thompson could sense their renewed commitment to promoting equity and inclusion as they worked together to foster a positive school culture. By emphasizing the importance of equity in education, inclusive practices, sustainability, and continuous learning and growth, she had equipped her team with the tools and mindset needed to create a school community where every member felt valued, respected, and empowered to thrive. She knew that with their collective effort and dedication, they would create a school community that served as a beacon of equity, inclusion, and excellence for all.

Engaging Families and the Community

Dr. Thompson seamlessly transitioned into the next subpoint of her discussion on fostering a positive school culture, emphasizing the vital role of engaging families and the community as partners in their educational journey. Assembled once again in the school auditorium, the faculty listened attentively, ready to explore the ways in which they could strengthen their relationships with families and the broader community to create a more vibrant and supportive learning environment.

"Good morning, everyone," Dr. Thompson greeted warmly, her voice exuding enthusiasm and warmth. "Today, we're diving into the transformative power of engaging families and the community in shaping our school culture. As leaders, it's essential that we build strong partnerships with families and community stakeholders to support the success of every student."

She clicked to the first slide, which displayed images of families, community events, and collaborative partnerships. "Engaging families and the community is not just about involvement; it's about building meaningful relationships based on trust, communication, and mutual respect," she began. "It's about recognizing that education is a shared responsibility that extends beyond the walls of our school."

Dr. Thompson emphasized the importance of **Family Engagement**. "Family engagement is a cornerstone of student success," she continued. "We'll create opportunities for families to actively participate in their child's education, from attending parent-teacher conferences to volunteering in the classroom. By fostering strong partnerships with families, we can create a supportive home-to-school connection that reinforces learning and promotes student achievement."

She moved on to **Community Collaboration**. "Community collaboration enriches our school culture and expands opportunities for our students," Dr. Thompson emphasized. "We'll collaborate with local businesses, organizations, and agencies to provide resources, mentorship, and real-world learning experiences for our students. By harnessing the collective expertise and resources of our community, we can broaden horizons and empower students to reach their full potential."

Mrs. Lee raised her hand. "Dr. Thompson, how do we ensure that our efforts to engage families and the community are inclusive and equitable?"

"An excellent question, Mrs. Lee," Dr. Thompson replied. "Ensuring inclusive and equitable family and community engagement requires intentionality, cultural competence, and a commitment to listening and learning from diverse perspectives. We'll engage with families and community members in culturally responsive ways, respecting their values, traditions, and lived experiences. By fostering an inclusive and equitable approach to family and community engagement, we can create a school community where everyone feels welcomed, valued, and empowered to contribute."

She clicked to the next slide, which displayed examples of family workshops, community partnerships, and multicultural events. "Our efforts towards engaging families and the community will be collaborative, culturally responsive, and focused on building strong relationships that support student success."

Finally, Dr. Thompson emphasized the importance of **Open Communication and Collaboration**. "Open communication and collaboration are essential for building trust and fostering meaningful partnerships," she concluded. "We'll create channels for two-way communication, seek feedback from families and community stakeholders, and collaborate on shared goals and initiatives. By working together as partners in education, we can create a school community where every member feels valued, supported, and empowered to thrive."

As the faculty members filed out of the auditorium, Dr. Thompson could sense their renewed commitment to engaging families and the community as partners in their educational journey. By emphasizing the importance of family engagement, community collaboration, inclusivity, and open communication, she had equipped her team with the tools and mindset needed to create a school community where every member felt valued, respected, and empowered to succeed. She knew that with their collective effort and dedication, they would create a school community that served as a beacon of collaboration, inclusivity, and excellence for all.

7

Chapter 7: Financial and Resource Management

Basics of School Finance and Budgeting

Dr. Thompson shifted the focus of her discussion to the critical topic of financial and resource management, starting with the fundamentals of school finance and budgeting. Assembled once more in the school auditorium, the faculty listened attentively, recognizing the importance of effective stewardship of resources in achieving their educational goals.

"Good afternoon, everyone," Dr. Thompson greeted, her voice poised and authoritative. "Today, we embark on a journey to explore the essentials of school finance and budgeting, essential components of our mission to provide quality education while ensuring fiscal responsibility."

She clicked to the first slide, displaying graphs and charts illustrating revenue sources and expenditure categories. "Understanding school finance begins with grasping the sources of

CHAPTER 7: FINANCIAL AND RESOURCE MANAGEMENT

funding and the allocation of resources," she began. "It's about making informed decisions to optimize the use of financial resources in support of our educational objectives."

Dr. Thompson emphasized the importance of **Revenue Sources**. "Revenue sources vary from state to state and district to district," she continued. "We'll explore the main sources of funding for our school, from local property taxes to state and federal allocations. By understanding where our funding comes from, we can better plan and allocate resources to meet the needs of our students and staff."

She moved on to **Budgeting Basics**. "Budgeting is the process of allocating resources to achieve specific goals and objectives," Dr. Thompson explained. "We'll delve into the principles of budgeting, from setting priorities and establishing spending limits to monitoring expenses and adjusting allocations as needed. By developing a clear and comprehensive budget, we can ensure that our financial resources are aligned with our strategic priorities and educational initiatives."

Mr. Harris raised his hand. "Dr. Thompson, how do we ensure transparency and accountability in our budgeting process?"

"An excellent question, Mr. Harris," Dr. Thompson replied. "Transparency and accountability are essential principles of effective financial management. We'll engage stakeholders in the budgeting process, communicate financial information openly and transparently, and establish mechanisms for oversight and review. By fostering a culture of transparency and accountability, we can build trust and confidence in our financial stewardship."

She clicked to the next slide, which displayed examples of budget documents, financial reports, and stakeholder engagement activities. "Our approach to school finance and budgeting will be transparent, inclusive, and focused on achieving our educational objectives while ensuring fiscal responsibility."

Finally, Dr. Thompson emphasized the importance of **Strategic Resource Allocation**. "Strategic resource allocation is about aligning financial resources with our strategic priorities and educational goals," she concluded. "We'll prioritize investments that have the greatest impact on student learning and well-being, while also ensuring efficiency and sustainability. By strategically allocating resources, we can maximize the value of every dollar spent and deliver the best possible outcomes for our students and staff."

As the faculty members filed out of the auditorium, Dr. Thompson could sense their growing appreciation for the intricacies of school finance and budgeting. By emphasizing the importance of understanding revenue sources, budgeting basics, transparency and accountability, and strategic resource allocation, she had equipped her team with the knowledge and skills needed to effectively manage financial resources in support of their educational mission. She knew that with their collective effort and dedication, they would ensure that every dollar spent contributed to the success and well-being of their students and staff.

Aligning Resources with School Priorities

Dr. Thompson seamlessly transitioned into the next subpoint of her discussion on financial and resource management, emphasizing the critical importance of aligning resources with the strategic priorities of the school. Assembled once more in the school auditorium, the faculty listened intently, understanding that effective allocation of resources was key to achieving their educational goals.

"Good morning, everyone," Dr. Thompson greeted, her voice brimming with purpose and determination. "Today, we're diving into the essential task of aligning resources with our school's strategic priorities, ensuring that every dollar spent contributes to our mission of providing quality education and supporting student success."

She clicked to the first slide, displaying images representing the school's strategic priorities, from academic excellence to student well-being. "Aligning resources with school priorities requires a strategic and intentional approach," she began. "It's about identifying our key objectives and allocating resources in a way that maximizes their impact on student learning and achievement."

Dr. Thompson emphasized the importance of **Strategic Planning**. "Strategic planning provides a roadmap for aligning resources with our school's priorities," she continued. "We'll assess our strengths, weaknesses, opportunities, and threats, identify our strategic priorities, and develop action plans to achieve our goals. By aligning our resource allocation decisions with our strategic plan, we can ensure that every investment supports our overarching objectives."

She moved on to **Resource Allocation Strategies**. "Resource allocation strategies determine how we distribute financial and human resources to meet the needs of our students and staff," Dr. Thompson explained. "We'll explore different models and approaches to resource allocation, from weighted student funding formulas to site-based budgeting. By selecting the right allocation strategies for our school context, we can optimize the use of resources and maximize their impact on student outcomes."

Mrs. Lee raised her hand. "Dr. Thompson, how do we prioritize competing needs and interests when allocating resources?"

"An excellent question, Mrs. Lee," Dr. Thompson replied. "Prioritizing competing needs requires collaboration, data analysis, and a clear understanding of our strategic priorities. We'll engage stakeholders in the decision-making process, gather input and feedback, and use data to inform our resource allocation decisions. By prioritizing investments that align with our strategic goals and have the greatest impact on student success, we can ensure that our resources are used effectively and efficiently."

She clicked to the next slide, which displayed examples of resource allocation frameworks, decision-making matrices, and stakeholder engagement activities. "Our approach to aligning resources with school priorities will be strategic, collaborative, and focused on achieving our educational objectives."

Finally, Dr. Thompson emphasized the importance of **Continuous Monitoring and Evaluation**. "Continuous monitoring and evaluation are essential for ensuring that our resource allocation decisions are effective and responsive to changing needs," she concluded. "We'll regularly assess the impact of our investments, gather feedback from stakeholders, and adjust our resource allocation strategies as needed. By committing to continuous improvement, we can ensure that our resources are directed towards activities that have the greatest impact on student learning and success."

As the faculty members filed out of the auditorium, Dr. Thompson could sense their growing confidence in their ability to align resources with school priorities. By emphasizing the importance of strategic planning, resource allocation strategies, stakeholder engagement, and continuous monitoring and evaluation, she had equipped her team with the knowledge and tools needed to make informed decisions that would benefit their students and school community. She knew that with their collective effort and dedication, they would ensure that every resource was directed towards supporting student success and achieving their shared vision of excellence.

Strategies for Efficient Resource Management

Dr. Thompson seamlessly transitioned into the next subpoint of her discussion on financial and resource management, highlighting the importance of implementing strategies for efficient resource management to maximize the impact of available resources. Assembled once more in the school auditorium, the faculty listened intently, recognizing the significance of optimizing their resources to better support their educational mission.

"Good afternoon, everyone," Dr. Thompson greeted, her voice infused with energy and determination. "Today, we're delving into the essential strategies for efficient resource management, ensuring that we make the most of our available resources to support student learning and achievement."

She clicked to the first slide, displaying images representing budgeting tools, resource allocation models, and efficiency measures. "Efficient resource management is about using our resources wisely and strategically," she began. "It's about finding ways to do more with less, without compromising the quality of education we provide."

Dr. Thompson emphasized the importance of **Data-**

Informed Decision Making. "Data provides valuable insights that can inform our resource allocation decisions," she continued. "We'll collect and analyze data on student performance, demographic trends, resource utilization, and other key metrics to identify areas for improvement and opportunities for efficiency gains. By basing our decisions on data, we can allocate resources more effectively and target interventions where they are needed most."

She moved on to **Collaborative Planning and Coordination.** "Collaboration is essential for efficient resource management," Dr. Thompson explained. "We'll work closely with staff, administrators, and stakeholders to develop coordinated plans and strategies for resource allocation. By leveraging the collective expertise and insights of our school community, we can identify creative solutions, streamline processes, and maximize the impact of our resources."

Mr. Harris raised his hand. "Dr. Thompson, how do we ensure that our resource management strategies are sustainable in the long term?"

"An excellent question, Mr. Harris," Dr. Thompson replied. "Sustainability requires careful planning, monitoring, and adaptation. We'll develop long-term plans and strategies that prioritize sustainability and resilience, taking into account future needs, challenges, and opportunities. By regularly reviewing and adjusting our resource management practices, we can ensure that our resources remain aligned with our evolving priorities and goals."

She clicked to the next slide, which displayed examples of efficiency measures, cost-saving initiatives, and collaborative planning processes. "Our approach to resource management will be strategic, data-driven, and collaborative, focused on maximizing the impact of our resources on student learning and achievement."

Finally, Dr. Thompson emphasized the importance of **Continuous Improvement**. "Continuous improvement is essential for ensuring that our resource management strategies remain effective and responsive to changing needs," she concluded. "We'll regularly evaluate our processes, gather feedback from stakeholders, and implement changes as needed to enhance efficiency and effectiveness. By committing to continuous improvement, we can ensure that our resources are used in the most efficient and impactful way possible."

As the faculty members filed out of the auditorium, Dr. Thompson could sense their growing confidence in their ability to manage resources efficiently. By emphasizing the importance of data-informed decision making, collaborative planning and coordination, sustainability, and continuous improvement, she had equipped her team with the knowledge and tools needed to make the most of their available resources. She knew that with their collective effort and dedication, they would ensure that every resource was used effectively to support student success and advance their school's mission.

Fundraising and Grant Writing

Dr. Thompson smoothly transitioned into the next subpoint of her discussion on financial and resource management, highlighting the significance of fundraising and grant writing as essential avenues for acquiring additional resources to support the school's objectives. Gathered once more in the school auditorium, the faculty listened attentively, recognizing the importance of exploring alternative sources of funding to enhance their educational initiatives.

"Good morning, everyone," Dr. Thompson greeted, her voice vibrant with enthusiasm and determination. "Today, we're exploring the valuable opportunities presented by fundraising and grant writing to secure additional resources for our school's mission."

She clicked to the first slide, displaying images showcasing successful fundraising events, grant awards, and community partnerships. "Fundraising and grant writing are essential strategies for supplementing our existing resources and expanding our capacity to support student learning and achievement," she began. "It's about tapping into external sources of funding to enhance our educational programs, facilities, and resources."

Dr. Thompson emphasized the importance of **Strategic Fundraising**. "Strategic fundraising involves identifying our fundraising priorities and developing targeted initiatives to support those priorities," she continued. "We'll explore a variety of fundraising strategies, from traditional events like bake sales and auctions to innovative approaches like crowdfunding campaigns and corporate sponsorships. By aligning our fundraising efforts with our strategic goals, we can maximize our impact and attract support from donors who share our vision."

She moved on to **Grant Writing Essentials**. "Grant writing is a specialized skill that requires careful planning, research, and writing," Dr. Thompson explained. "We'll learn the fundamentals of grant writing, from identifying funding opportunities to crafting compelling proposals that effectively communicate our needs, goals, and strategies. By mastering the art of grant writing, we can access funding from government agencies, foundations, and other organizations to support our initiatives."

Mrs. Lee raised her hand. "Dr. Thompson, how do we ensure that our fundraising and grant writing efforts are successful?"

"An excellent question, Mrs. Lee," Dr. Thompson replied. "Successful fundraising and grant writing require a strategic and collaborative approach. We'll engage stakeholders in the process, solicit input and feedback, and leverage our collective networks and resources to maximize our chances of success. By building relationships with potential donors and funders, articulating our needs and priorities effectively, and demonstrating the impact of our work, we can increase our chances of securing funding to support our school's mission."

She clicked to the next slide, which displayed examples of successful fundraising campaigns, grant proposals, and donor recognition initiatives. "Our approach to fundraising and grant writing will be strategic, collaborative, and focused on enhancing our capacity to support student learning and achievement."

Finally, Dr. Thompson emphasized the importance of **Stewardship and Accountability**. "Stewardship and accountability are essential principles of effective fundraising and grant management," she concluded. "We'll ensure that funds raised are used responsibly and transparently, with clear accountability mechanisms in place to track and report on our use of resources. By demonstrating good stewardship and accountability, we can build trust and confidence with our donors and funders, ensuring continued support for our school's mission."

As the faculty members filed out of the auditorium, Dr. Thompson could sense their growing enthusiasm for exploring new avenues of funding to support their educational initiatives. By emphasizing the importance of strategic fundraising, grant writing essentials, collaboration, and stewardship, she had equipped her team with the knowledge and skills needed to leverage external resources to enhance their capacity to support student success. She knew that with their collective effort and dedication, they would secure the additional funding needed to advance their school's mission and provide even greater opportunities for their students.

Transparency and Accountability in Financial Management

Dr. Thompson seamlessly transitioned into the next sub-point of her discussion on financial and resource management, highlighting the critical importance of transparency and accountability in ensuring responsible stewardship of the school's financial resources. Gathered once again in the school auditorium, the faculty listened attentively, recognizing the significance of maintaining trust and integrity in financial matters.

"Good afternoon, everyone," Dr. Thompson greeted, her voice resonating with sincerity and integrity. "Today, we delve into the essential principles of transparency and accountability in financial management, foundational elements of our commitment to responsible stewardship and ethical conduct."

She clicked to the first slide, displaying images depicting financial reports, budget summaries, and transparency measures. "Transparency is about openness and honesty in our financial practices," she began. "It's about providing clear, accurate, and timely information to stakeholders, so they can understand how our resources are being used and make informed decisions."

Dr. Thompson emphasized the importance of **Clear Communication**. "Clear communication is key to fostering transparency," she continued. "We'll provide regular updates on our financial status, budget allocations, and expenditures through newsletters, meetings, and online platforms. By keeping stakeholders informed, we can build trust and confidence in our financial management practices."

She moved on to **Accountability Measures**. "Accountability holds us accountable for our actions and decisions," Dr. Thompson explained. "We'll establish mechanisms for oversight, review, and audit to ensure that our financial practices are in line with regulations and best practices. By holding ourselves to high standards of accountability, we can demonstrate our commitment to ethical conduct and responsible stewardship."

Mr. Harris raised his hand. "Dr. Thompson, how do we ensure that our financial management practices are transparent and accountable?"

"An excellent question, Mr. Harris," Dr. Thompson replied. "Ensuring transparency and accountability requires a proactive and systematic approach. We'll implement policies and procedures that promote transparency, such as open budget meetings, financial reports, and regular audits. We'll also establish channels for feedback and complaints, so stakeholders can raise concerns and provide input on our financial management practices. By creating a culture of transparency and accountability, we can build trust and confidence in our financial stewardship."

She clicked to the next slide, which displayed examples

of transparency measures, accountability mechanisms, and stakeholder engagement activities. "Our commitment to transparency and accountability will be unwavering, as we strive to uphold the highest standards of integrity and trustworthiness in all our financial dealings."

Finally, Dr. Thompson emphasized the importance of **Continuous Improvement**. "Continuous improvement is essential for ensuring that our financial management practices remain effective and responsive to changing needs and expectations," she concluded. "We'll regularly review and evaluate our policies and procedures, gather feedback from stakeholders, and implement changes as needed to enhance transparency and accountability. By committing to continuous improvement, we can ensure that our financial management practices evolve to meet the needs of our school community."

As the faculty members filed out of the auditorium, Dr. Thompson could sense their renewed commitment to transparency and accountability in financial management. By emphasizing the importance of clear communication, accountability measures, proactive oversight, and continuous improvement, she had equipped her team with the knowledge and tools needed to uphold the highest standards of integrity and trustworthiness in their financial practices. She knew that with their collective effort and dedication, they would ensure that every dollar spent was used responsibly and ethically to support student success and advance their school's mission.

Long-Term Financial Planning

Dr. Thompson smoothly transitioned into the next subpoint of her discussion on financial and resource management, emphasizing the importance of long-term financial planning in ensuring the sustainability and resilience of the school's financial health. The faculty, gathered once more in the school auditorium, listened attentively, recognizing the significance of preparing for the future to safeguard the school's mission and objectives.

"Good morning, everyone," Dr. Thompson greeted, her voice conveying foresight and prudence. "Today, we explore the critical importance of long-term financial planning, an essential component of our commitment to securing the financial well-being of our school both now and in the future."

She clicked to the first slide, displaying images depicting financial forecasts, investment strategies, and fiscal projections. "Long-term financial planning is about taking a proactive and strategic approach to managing our financial resources," she began. "It's about anticipating future needs, challenges, and opportunities and developing plans and strategies to address them effectively."

Dr. Thompson emphasized the importance of **Strategic Forecasting**. "Strategic forecasting enables us to anticipate changes in our financial landscape and prepare accordingly," she continued. "We'll analyze trends, projections, and economic indicators to forecast revenue, expenses, and funding sources over the long term. By understanding the financial implications of various scenarios, we can make informed decisions and develop strategies to mitigate risks and capitalize on opportunities."

She moved on to **Risk Management**. "Risk management is an integral part of long-term financial planning," Dr. Thompson explained. "We'll identify potential risks and uncertainties that could impact our financial health, such as enrollment fluctuations, changes in funding levels, or economic downturns. By developing risk mitigation strategies and contingency plans, we can safeguard our financial stability and resilience in the face of uncertainty."

Mrs. Lee raised her hand. "Dr. Thompson, how do we ensure that our long-term financial planning is aligned with our strategic goals and priorities?"

"An excellent question, Mrs. Lee," Dr. Thompson replied. "Aligning long-term financial planning with our strategic goals requires collaboration, communication, and a clear understanding of our priorities. We'll engage stakeholders in the planning process, solicit input and feedback, and ensure that our financial priorities are aligned with our educational objectives. By integrating financial planning into our strategic planning process, we can ensure that our financial resources are directed towards activities that support our mission and vision."

She clicked to the next slide, which displayed examples of long-term financial plans, scenario analyses, and strategic alignment matrices. "Our approach to long-term financial planning will be proactive, collaborative, and focused on securing the financial health and sustainability of our school."

Finally, Dr. Thompson emphasized the importance of **Flexibility and Adaptability**. "Flexibility and adaptability are essential for successful long-term financial planning," she concluded. "We'll regularly review and update our financial plans in response to changing circumstances, new information, and emerging priorities. By remaining agile and responsive, we can ensure that our financial strategies remain relevant and effective in an ever-changing environment."

As the faculty members filed out of the auditorium, Dr. Thompson could sense their growing appreciation for the importance of long-term financial planning in safeguarding the school's mission and objectives. By emphasizing the importance of strategic forecasting, risk management, alignment with strategic goals, and flexibility and adaptability, she had equipped her team with the knowledge and tools needed to navigate the complexities of long-term financial management. She knew that with their collective effort and dedication, they would ensure the financial health and sustainability of their school for years to come.

8

Chapter 8: Leveraging Technology in Education

Role of Technology in Modern Education

Dr. Thompson shifted the focus of her discussion to the transformative role of technology in modern education, highlighting its potential to enhance teaching and learning experiences. Assembled once more in the school auditorium, the faculty listened attentively, recognizing the significance of integrating technology to meet the evolving needs of their students in the digital age.

"Good afternoon, everyone," Dr. Thompson greeted, her voice vibrant with excitement and anticipation. "Today, we embark on a journey to explore the powerful role of technology in modern education, revolutionizing the way we teach, learn, and engage with knowledge."

She clicked to the first slide, displaying images depicting classrooms equipped with interactive whiteboards, students collaborating on tablets, and teachers using educational apps.

CHAPTER 8: LEVERAGING TECHNOLOGY IN EDUCATION

"Technology has become an integral part of our daily lives, transforming how we communicate, work, and learn," she began. "In education, technology serves as a catalyst for innovation, enabling us to create more interactive, personalized, and immersive learning experiences for our students."

Dr. Thompson emphasized the importance of **Enhancing Learning Experiences**. "Technology offers endless possibilities for enhancing learning experiences," she continued. "From interactive multimedia resources and virtual simulations to online collaboration tools and adaptive learning platforms, technology empowers us to engage students in more meaningful and effective ways. By leveraging technology, we can cater to diverse learning styles, interests, and abilities, making learning more accessible, engaging, and relevant."

She moved on to **Facilitating Access to Information**. "Technology provides unprecedented access to information and resources," Dr. Thompson explained. "With the click of a button, students can access vast repositories of knowledge, explore multimedia content, and connect with experts and peers from around the world. By leveraging technology to expand access to information, we can empower students to become independent, lifelong learners who are equipped to thrive in the digital age."

Mr. Harris raised his hand. "Dr. Thompson, how do we ensure that technology is used effectively to support learning goals?"

"An excellent question, Mr. Harris," Dr. Thompson replied. "Effective technology integration requires careful planning, training, and ongoing support. We'll align technology use with our learning goals and objectives, provide professional development opportunities for teachers, and ensure that technology is integrated seamlessly into our curriculum. By fostering a culture of innovation and collaboration, we can maximize the educational potential of technology and ensure that it enhances, rather than detracts from, student learning."

She clicked to the next slide, which displayed examples of technology-enhanced learning activities, professional development workshops, and student engagement initiatives. "Our approach to leveraging technology in education will be strategic, intentional, and focused on enhancing learning outcomes for all students."

Finally, Dr. Thompson emphasized the importance of **Equity and Access**. "Equity and access are essential considerations in technology integration," she concluded. "We'll ensure that all students have access to technology and digital resources, regardless of their background or circumstances. By addressing barriers to access and providing support for students who may lack access to technology outside of school, we can ensure that technology serves as a tool for empowerment and inclusion, rather than a source of inequity."

As the faculty members filed out of the auditorium, Dr. Thompson could sense their growing enthusiasm for leveraging technology to enhance teaching and learning experiences. By emphasizing the importance of enhancing learning experiences, facilitating access to information, effective technology use, and equity and access, she had equipped her team with the knowledge and tools needed to harness the power of technology to support student success and prepare them for the challenges and opportunities of the digital age. She knew that with their collective effort and dedication, they would create a learning environment where technology served as a catalyst for innovation, engagement, and achievement.

Integrating Technology into the Curriculum

Dr. Thompson seamlessly transitioned into the next subpoint of her discussion on leveraging technology in education, highlighting the importance of integrating technology into the curriculum to enhance teaching and learning experiences. The faculty, gathered once more in the school auditorium, listened attentively, recognizing the significance of embedding technology seamlessly into their instructional practices.

"Good morning, everyone," Dr. Thompson greeted, her voice brimming with enthusiasm and purpose. "Today, we delve into the essential task of integrating technology into the curriculum, transforming our instructional practices and enriching the learning experiences of our students."

She clicked to the first slide, displaying images depicting classrooms bustling with activity, students collaborating on digital projects, and teachers leading interactive lessons using technology. "Integrating technology into the curriculum is about more than just using digital tools," she began. "It's about leveraging technology to enhance and extend our teaching and learning practices, fostering creativity, critical thinking, and collaboration among our students."

Dr. Thompson emphasized the importance of **Curriculum Alignment**. "Curriculum alignment ensures that technology use is purposeful and meaningful," she continued. "We'll identify learning objectives and standards that lend themselves to technology integration, align digital resources and activities with our curriculum goals, and design authentic, inquiry-based learning experiences that leverage the affordances of technology. By integrating technology seamlessly into our curriculum, we can enhance student engagement and achievement across all subject areas."

She moved on to **Differentiated Instruction**. "Technology enables us to personalize learning experiences to meet the diverse needs and interests of our students," Dr. Thompson explained. "We'll leverage digital tools and resources to provide individualized instruction, adaptive feedback, and tailored learning pathways that support students at their own pace and level. By embracing differentiated instruction, we can empower every student to reach their full potential and succeed in their learning journey."

Mrs. Lee raised her hand. "Dr. Thompson, how do we ensure that technology integration enhances, rather than detracts from, our curriculum?"

"An excellent question, Mrs. Lee," Dr. Thompson replied. "Effective technology integration requires careful planning, pedagogical alignment, and ongoing reflection. We'll provide professional development opportunities for teachers to explore best practices for integrating technology into their instructional practices, model exemplary uses of technology in the classroom, and create opportunities for collaboration and peer learning. By fostering a culture of innovation and inquiry, we can ensure that technology enhances, enriches, and extends our curriculum in meaningful ways."

She clicked to the next slide, which displayed examples of technology-integrated lesson plans, student projects, and collaborative learning activities. "Our approach to integrating technology into the curriculum will be strategic, intentional, and focused on enhancing learning outcomes for all students."

Finally, Dr. Thompson emphasized the importance of **Continuous Improvement**. "Continuous improvement is essential for ensuring that technology integration remains effective and responsive to changing needs and expectations," she concluded. "We'll regularly evaluate our practices, gather feedback from stakeholders, and implement changes as needed to enhance the quality and impact of technology integration. By committing to continuous improvement, we can ensure that technology enhances, rather than detracts from, the richness and depth of our curriculum."

As the faculty members filed out of the auditorium, Dr. Thompson could sense their growing enthusiasm for integrating technology into the curriculum. By emphasizing the importance of curriculum alignment, differentiated instruction, effective technology use, and continuous improvement, she had equipped her team with the knowledge and tools needed to leverage technology to enhance teaching and learning experiences. She knew that with their collective effort and dedication, they would create a curriculum that embraced the transformative potential of technology, empowering students to thrive in the digital age.

Supporting Teachers in Technology Use

Dr. Thompson seamlessly transitioned into the next subpoint of her discussion on leveraging technology in education, emphasizing the critical importance of supporting teachers in effectively integrating technology into their instructional practices. Assembled once more in the school auditorium, the faculty listened attentively, recognizing the significance of providing teachers with the necessary tools and training to harness the power of technology in the classroom.

"Good afternoon, everyone," Dr. Thompson greeted, her voice filled with warmth and encouragement. "Today, we turn our attention to the vital task of supporting teachers in technology use, empowering them to leverage digital tools and resources to enhance their teaching and enrich student learning experiences."

She clicked to the first slide, displaying images depicting teachers engaged in professional development workshops, collaborating on digital projects, and receiving one-on-one coaching on technology integration. "Supporting teachers in technology use is essential for successful technology integration," she began. "It's about providing teachers with the knowledge, skills, and resources they need to effectively integrate technology into their instructional practices and maximize its impact on student learning."

Dr. Thompson emphasized the importance of **Professional Development**. "Professional development plays a crucial role in supporting teachers in technology use," she continued. "We'll offer a variety of professional development opportunities, from workshops and seminars to online courses and coaching sessions, tailored to meet the diverse needs and interests of our teachers. By providing ongoing support and training, we can help teachers build confidence and competence in using technology to enhance their teaching."

She moved on to **Coaching and Mentoring**. "Coaching and mentoring provide personalized support for teachers as they integrate technology into their instructional practices," Dr. Thompson explained. "We'll pair teachers with technology coaches or mentors who can provide guidance, feedback, and encouragement as they explore new digital tools and strategies. By offering individualized support and feedback, we can help teachers overcome challenges, build their skills, and develop innovative approaches to teaching with technology."

Mr. Harris raised his hand. "Dr. Thompson, how do we ensure that professional development and support are aligned with teachers' needs and interests?"

"An excellent question, Mr. Harris," Dr. Thompson replied. "Effective professional development starts with understanding teachers' needs, interests, and goals. We'll conduct needs assessments, gather feedback from teachers, and tailor professional development opportunities to meet their specific needs and interests. By providing relevant, timely, and differentiated support, we can ensure that teachers have the resources and encouragement they need to succeed in integrating technology into their teaching."

She clicked to the next slide, which displayed examples of professional development workshops, coaching sessions, and teacher-led technology initiatives. "Our approach to supporting teachers in technology use will be collaborative, personalized, and focused on empowering teachers to harness the full potential of technology to enhance their teaching and enrich student learning experiences."

Finally, Dr. Thompson emphasized the importance of **Sustained Support**. "Sustained support is essential for ensuring that teachers continue to grow and develop as technology users," she concluded. "We'll provide ongoing opportunities for collaboration, reflection, and learning, creating a culture of continuous improvement and innovation. By fostering a supportive and dynamic learning community, we can empower teachers to embrace technology as a powerful tool for transforming teaching and learning."

As the faculty members filed out of the auditorium, Dr. Thompson could sense their growing enthusiasm for supporting teachers in technology use. By emphasizing the importance of professional development, coaching and mentoring, alignment with teachers' needs and interests, and sustained support, she had equipped her team with the knowledge and tools needed to effectively integrate technology into their instructional practices. She knew that with their collective effort and dedication, they would create a learning environment where technology served as a catalyst for innovation, collaboration, and student success.

Ensuring Digital Equity and Access

Dr. Thompson seamlessly transitioned into the next subpoint of her discussion on leveraging technology in education, emphasizing the critical importance of ensuring digital equity and access for all students. Assembled once more in the school auditorium, the faculty listened attentively, recognizing the significance of providing equal opportunities for all students to benefit from technology-enhanced learning experiences.

"Good morning, everyone," Dr. Thompson greeted, her voice resonating with determination and inclusivity. "Today, we address the pressing need to ensure digital equity and access, ensuring that all students have the opportunity to benefit from the transformative potential of technology in education."

She clicked to the first slide, displaying images depicting students from diverse backgrounds engaging with digital devices and resources. "Digital equity is about more than just access to technology," she began. "It's about ensuring that all students, regardless of their background or circumstances, have access to the digital tools, resources, and opportunities they need to succeed in the digital age."

Dr. Thompson emphasized the importance of **Closing**

the Digital Divide. "The digital divide refers to the gap between those who have access to technology and those who do not," she continued. "We'll work tirelessly to close this divide by providing equitable access to technology and digital resources for all students. This may involve providing devices and internet access to students who lack them, offering technology loans or subsidies, and partnering with community organizations to expand access to digital resources beyond the school walls."

She moved on to **Addressing Barriers to Access**. "Barriers to access go beyond physical devices and internet connectivity," Dr. Thompson explained. "They may include factors such as language barriers, disabilities, or lack of digital literacy skills. We'll identify and address these barriers by providing multilingual support, accommodations for students with disabilities, and targeted interventions to build digital literacy skills. By addressing barriers to access, we can ensure that all students have the opportunity to engage meaningfully with technology and benefit from its potential to enhance learning."

Mrs. Lee raised her hand. "Dr. Thompson, how do we ensure that our efforts to promote digital equity are sustainable and inclusive?"

"An excellent question, Mrs. Lee," Dr. Thompson replied. "Sustainable and inclusive digital equity requires a comprehensive and systemic approach. We'll embed equity considerations into all aspects of our technology integration efforts, from procurement and policy development to curriculum design and professional development. By prioritizing equity and inclusion in our decision-making processes, we can create a learning environment where all students feel valued, supported, and empowered to succeed."

She clicked to the next slide, which displayed examples of initiatives to promote digital equity and access, including device distribution programs, digital literacy workshops, and community partnerships. "Our commitment to digital equity and access will be unwavering, as we strive to create a more equitable and inclusive learning environment for all students."

Finally, Dr. Thompson emphasized the importance of **Community Engagement**. "Community engagement is essential for promoting digital equity and access," she concluded. "We'll collaborate with parents, community organizations, and other stakeholders to raise awareness, gather input, and mobilize resources to support our efforts. By working together with our community, we can create a more equitable and inclusive learning ecosystem where all students have the opportunity to thrive."

As the faculty members filed out of the auditorium, Dr. Thompson could sense their renewed commitment to promoting digital equity and access. By emphasizing the importance of closing the digital divide, addressing barriers to access, sustainability, and community engagement, she had equipped her team with the knowledge and tools needed to ensure that all students had equal opportunities to benefit from technology-enhanced learning experiences. She knew that with their collective effort and dedication, they would create a more equitable and inclusive learning environment where every student could reach their full potential.

Managing Cybersecurity and Data Privacy

Dr. Thompson smoothly transitioned into the next subpoint of her discussion on leveraging technology in education, emphasizing the critical importance of managing cybersecurity and data privacy to protect students' sensitive information. Assembled once more in the school auditorium, the faculty listened attentively, recognizing the significance of safeguarding digital assets and maintaining trust with students, parents, and the community.

"Good afternoon, everyone," Dr. Thompson greeted, her voice imbued with a sense of responsibility and vigilance. "Today, we address the vital task of managing cybersecurity and data privacy, ensuring the safety and security of our students' digital information in an increasingly connected world."

She clicked to the first slide, displaying images depicting secure network connections, encrypted data, and cybersecurity protocols. "Cybersecurity is a growing concern in education, with schools facing increasing threats from cyberattacks, data breaches, and other malicious activities," she began. "It's imperative that we take proactive measures to protect our digital assets and safeguard the privacy and security of our students' sensitive information."

Dr. Thompson emphasized the importance of **Implementing Robust Security Measures**. "Robust security measures are essential for protecting against cybersecurity threats," she continued. "We'll implement measures such as firewalls, encryption, multi-factor authentication, and regular security audits to safeguard our network infrastructure and prevent unauthorized access to sensitive information. By staying vigilant and proactive, we can mitigate the risk of cyberattacks and ensure the integrity and confidentiality of our data."

She moved on to **Promoting Data Privacy**. "Data privacy is equally important for protecting students' sensitive information," Dr. Thompson explained. "We'll establish clear policies and procedures for data collection, storage, and sharing, ensuring that student data is collected and used responsibly and ethically. We'll also provide training and guidance for staff on best practices for data privacy and security, empowering them to handle student data with care and respect."

Mr. Harris raised his hand. "Dr. Thompson, how do we ensure that our cybersecurity measures are effective and up to date?"

"An excellent question, Mr. Harris," Dr. Thompson replied. "Effective cybersecurity requires a proactive and continuous approach. We'll stay informed about emerging threats and trends in cybersecurity, regularly update our security measures and protocols, and conduct regular security assessments and audits to identify and address vulnerabilities. By remaining vigilant and responsive, we can ensure that our cybersecurity measures are effective and up to date."

She clicked to the next slide, which displayed examples of cybersecurity protocols, data privacy policies, and staff training initiatives. "Our approach to managing cybersecurity and data privacy will be comprehensive, proactive, and focused on protecting our students' sensitive information and maintaining trust with our school community."

Finally, Dr. Thompson emphasized the importance of **Transparency and Communication**. "Transparency and communication are essential for building trust and confidence with our students, parents, and the community," she concluded. "We'll communicate openly and transparently about our cybersecurity and data privacy practices, providing regular updates and opportunities for feedback. By fostering a culture of transparency and accountability, we can reassure our stakeholders that we take their privacy and security seriously and are committed to protecting their digital information."

As the faculty members filed out of the auditorium, Dr. Thompson could sense their growing awareness of the importance of managing cybersecurity and data privacy in education. By emphasizing the importance of robust security measures, data privacy, effectiveness and up-to-date measures, transparency and communication, she had equipped her team with the knowledge and tools needed to safeguard students' sensitive information and maintain trust with their school community. She knew that with their collective effort and dedication, they would create a safe and secure digital learning environment where students could thrive and succeed.

Evaluating the Impact of Technology on Learning

Dr. Thompson smoothly transitioned into the next subpoint of her discussion on leveraging technology in education, emphasizing the importance of evaluating the impact of technology on learning outcomes. Assembled once more in the school auditorium, the faculty listened attentively, recognizing the significance of assessing the effectiveness of their technology integration efforts to inform future decision-making and improve instructional practices.

"Good morning, everyone," Dr. Thompson greeted, her voice infused with a sense of curiosity and inquiry. "Today, we embark on the crucial task of evaluating the impact of technology on learning, gaining insights into how digital tools and resources are enhancing student engagement, achievement, and overall learning experiences."

She clicked to the first slide, displaying images depicting students using technology in various learning environments, engaged in collaborative projects, and exploring digital resources. "Evaluating the impact of technology on learning is essential for ensuring that our technology integration efforts are effective and aligned with our educational goals," she began. "It's about measuring the extent to which technology enhances teaching and learning experiences, informs instructional practices, and improves student outcomes."

Dr. Thompson emphasized the importance of **Data Collection and Analysis**. "Data collection and analysis are fundamental to evaluating the impact of technology on learning," she continued. "We'll gather data on various aspects of technology integration, including usage patterns, student engagement, academic performance, and teacher practices. By analyzing this data, we can identify trends, patterns, and correlations that provide insights into the effectiveness of our technology integration efforts."

She moved on to **Stakeholder Feedback**. "Stakeholder feedback is also invaluable for evaluating the impact of technology on learning," Dr. Thompson explained. "We'll solicit feedback from students, teachers, parents, and other stakeholders through surveys, interviews, focus groups, and observation. By gathering diverse perspectives and experiences, we can gain a holistic understanding of how technology is influencing teaching and learning experiences from multiple angles."

Mrs. Lee raised her hand. "Dr. Thompson, how do we ensure that our evaluation efforts are meaningful and actionable?"

"An excellent question, Mrs. Lee," Dr. Thompson replied.

"Meaningful evaluation requires clear goals, appropriate measures, and actionable insights. We'll establish clear evaluation criteria and benchmarks aligned with our educational goals, use a mix of quantitative and qualitative measures to capture the multifaceted nature of technology's impact on learning, and involve stakeholders in interpreting and applying the findings. By ensuring that our evaluation efforts are rigorous, relevant, and responsive, we can use the insights gained to inform future decision-making and improve instructional practices."

She clicked to the next slide, which displayed examples of evaluation frameworks, data collection tools, and stakeholder feedback mechanisms. "Our approach to evaluating the impact of technology on learning will be comprehensive, systematic, and focused on continuous improvement."

Finally, Dr. Thompson emphasized the importance of **Continuous Improvement**. "Continuous improvement is at the heart of our evaluation efforts," she concluded. "We'll use the insights gained from our evaluations to identify strengths, weaknesses, and areas for improvement in our technology integration efforts, and develop strategies and interventions to address them. By committing to continuous learning and adaptation, we can ensure that technology continues to enhance teaching and learning experiences for all students."

As the faculty members filed out of the auditorium, Dr. Thompson could sense their growing appreciation for the importance of evaluating the impact of technology on learning. By emphasizing the importance of data collection and analysis, stakeholder feedback, meaningful evaluation, and continuous improvement, she had equipped her team with the knowledge and tools needed to assess the effectiveness of their technology integration efforts and ensure that technology continued to enhance teaching and learning experiences for all students. She knew that with their collective effort and dedication, they would create a learning environment where technology served as a powerful tool for innovation, engagement, and student success.

9

Chapter 9: Legal and Ethical Issues in Educational Leadership

Understanding Educational Laws and Policies

Dr. Thompson shifted the focus of her discussion to the intricate landscape of legal and ethical issues in educational leadership, emphasizing the importance of understanding educational laws and policies. Assembled once more in the school auditorium, the faculty listened attentively, recognizing the significance of navigating the complex legal framework governing education with integrity and diligence.

"Good afternoon, everyone," Dr. Thompson greeted, her voice carrying the weight of responsibility and accountability. "Today, we delve into the multifaceted realm of legal and ethical issues in educational leadership, beginning with the essential task of understanding educational laws and policies that shape our practice and decision-making."

She clicked to the first slide, displaying images depicting

statutes, regulations, and policy documents related to education. "Understanding educational laws and policies is fundamental to effective educational leadership," she began. "It's about ensuring compliance with legal requirements, protecting the rights and interests of students and staff, and upholding the principles of fairness, equity, and justice in our educational practices."

Dr. Thompson emphasized the importance of **Legal Compliance**. "Legal compliance involves adhering to federal, state, and local laws and regulations governing education," she continued. "We'll familiarize ourselves with key legal frameworks, such as the Individuals with Disabilities Education Act (IDEA), Title IX, and the Family Educational Rights and Privacy Act (FERPA), that outline the rights and responsibilities of students, educators, and educational institutions. By understanding and complying with these laws, we can ensure that our practices are lawful, ethical, and conducive to student success."

She moved on to **Policy Implementation**. "Policy implementation is equally important for effective educational leadership," Dr. Thompson explained. "We'll review and interpret school district policies and procedures, communicate them to staff and stakeholders, and ensure that they are implemented consistently and fairly across all aspects of our educational programs and operations. By aligning our practices with district policies, we can promote accountability, transparency, and equity in our educational leadership."

Mr. Harris raised his hand. "Dr. Thompson, how do we ensure that our practices are both legally compliant and ethically sound?"

"An excellent question, Mr. Harris," Dr. Thompson replied. "Ensuring both legal compliance and ethical integrity requires careful consideration of the broader ethical implications of our actions and decisions. We'll engage in ethical reflection and dialogue, consult with legal counsel and other experts as needed, and prioritize the well-being and best interests of our students and community in all that we do. By upholding high ethical standards and seeking to do what is right, rather than just what is legal, we can ensure that our leadership practices are both legally compliant and ethically sound."

She clicked to the next slide, which displayed examples of legal frameworks, policy documents, and ethical guidelines for educational leadership. "Our approach to understanding educational laws and policies will be comprehensive, proactive, and focused on promoting integrity and excellence in educational leadership."

Finally, Dr. Thompson emphasized the importance of **Continuous Learning and Adaptation**. "Continuous learning and adaptation are essential for staying informed about changes in educational laws and policies," she concluded. "We'll engage in ongoing professional development, attend training sessions and workshops, and stay abreast of legal updates and developments to ensure that our knowledge and practices remain current and relevant. By committing to continuous learning and adaptation, we can fulfill our responsibilities as educational leaders and uphold the principles of legality, fairness, and ethical integrity in all that we do."

As the faculty members filed out of the auditorium, Dr. Thompson could sense their growing appreciation for the importance of understanding educational laws and policies in educational leadership. By emphasizing the importance of legal compliance, policy implementation, ethical integrity, and continuous learning and adaptation, she had equipped her team with the knowledge and tools needed to navigate the complex legal and ethical landscape of educational leadership with confidence and integrity. She knew that with their collective effort and dedication, they would uphold the highest standards of legality, fairness, and ethical integrity in their leadership practices, ensuring the well-being and success of their students and community.

Navigating Ethical Dilemmas in Leadership

Dr. Thompson seamlessly transitioned into the next subpoint of her discussion on legal and ethical issues in educational leadership, emphasizing the importance of navigating ethical dilemmas with integrity and professionalism. Assembled once more in the school auditorium, the faculty listened attentively, recognizing the significance of upholding ethical principles in their leadership roles.

"Good morning, everyone," Dr. Thompson greeted, her voice resonating with solemnity and thoughtfulness. "Today, we confront the complex terrain of ethical dilemmas in educational leadership, grappling with challenging situations that require careful deliberation and ethical discernment."

She clicked to the first slide, displaying images depicting ethical decision-making frameworks, moral dilemmas, and ethical guidelines for educational leaders. "Ethical dilemmas are situations in which conflicting moral principles or values require us to make difficult choices," she began. "As educational leaders, we must navigate these dilemmas with integrity, transparency, and a steadfast commitment to ethical principles."

Dr. Thompson emphasized the importance of **Ethical Reflection**. "Ethical reflection involves critically examining our values, beliefs, and assumptions, and considering the ethical implications of our actions and decisions," she continued. "We'll engage in reflective practices, such as journaling, dialogue, and ethical decision-making exercises, to deepen our understanding of ethical issues and develop our moral reasoning skills. By engaging in ethical reflection, we can cultivate ethical awareness and sensitivity, enabling us to navigate ethical dilemmas with clarity and purpose."

She moved on to **Consultation and Collaboration**. "Consultation and collaboration are essential for effectively addressing ethical dilemmas," Dr. Thompson explained. "We'll seek input from colleagues, mentors, and trusted advisors, and engage in collaborative problem-solving processes to explore alternative perspectives and approaches. By involving others in our ethical deliberations, we can gain valuable insights, identify blind spots, and make more informed and ethical decisions."

Mrs. Lee raised her hand. "Dr. Thompson, how do we ensure that our decisions are ethically defensible and aligned with our values?"

"An excellent question, Mrs. Lee," Dr. Thompson replied. "Ensuring ethical defensibility requires us to align our decisions with our core values and ethical principles, such as integrity, fairness, and respect for others. We'll use ethical decision-making frameworks, such as the ethical principles approach or the ethical decision-making model, to systematically analyze ethical dilemmas, consider alternative courses of action, and evaluate the potential consequences of our decisions. By grounding our decisions in ethical principles and rigorous analysis, we can ensure that our actions are ethically defensible and consistent with our values."

She clicked to the next slide, which displayed examples of

ethical decision-making frameworks, case studies of ethical dilemmas, and guidelines for ethical leadership. "Our approach to navigating ethical dilemmas in leadership will be principled, reflective, and collaborative."

Finally, Dr. Thompson emphasized the importance of **Courage and Integrity**. "Courage and integrity are essential for ethical leadership," she concluded. "We'll have the courage to stand up for what is right, even in the face of opposition or adversity, and the integrity to uphold our ethical principles and values, even when it is difficult or unpopular. By demonstrating courage and integrity in our leadership, we can inspire trust, foster accountability, and uphold the highest ethical standards in our educational community."

As the faculty members filed out of the auditorium, Dr. Thompson could sense their growing appreciation for the importance of navigating ethical dilemmas in educational leadership. By emphasizing the importance of ethical reflection, consultation and collaboration, ethical defensibility, and courage and integrity, she had equipped her team with the knowledge and tools needed to navigate ethical challenges with wisdom, compassion, and integrity. She knew that with their collective effort and dedication, they would uphold the highest ethical standards and ensure the well-being and success of their students and community.

Ensuring Compliance with Legal Standards

Dr. Thompson smoothly transitioned into the next subpoint of her discussion on legal and ethical issues in educational leadership, emphasizing the critical importance of ensuring compliance with legal standards. Assembled once more in the school auditorium, the faculty listened attentively, recognizing the significance of upholding legal requirements to maintain the integrity and credibility of their educational institution.

"Good afternoon, everyone," Dr. Thompson greeted, her voice carrying a tone of seriousness and responsibility. "Today, we delve into the essential task of ensuring compliance with legal standards, navigating the complex legal landscape of education with diligence and integrity."

She clicked to the first slide, displaying images depicting legal documents, statutes, and regulations governing education. "Compliance with legal standards is paramount for educational leaders," she began. "It's about adhering to federal, state, and local laws and regulations that govern various aspects of education, including student rights, safety, privacy, and accessibility."

Dr. Thompson emphasized the importance of **Knowledge of Legal Requirements**. "Knowledge of legal requirements is foundational to ensuring compliance," she continued. "We'll familiarize ourselves with key laws and regulations, such as the Individuals with Disabilities Education Act (IDEA), Title IX, and the Every Student Succeeds Act (ESSA), that outline the rights and responsibilities of students, educators, and educational institutions. By staying informed about legal requirements, we can ensure that our practices and policies align with legal standards and obligations."

She moved on to **Policy Development and Implementation**. "Policy development and implementation are instrumental in ensuring compliance with legal standards," Dr. Thompson explained. "We'll develop clear and comprehensive policies and procedures that reflect legal requirements and best practices, and ensure that they are effectively communicated, implemented, and enforced throughout our educational institution. By establishing robust policies and procedures, we can promote consistency, fairness, and accountability in our practices."

Mr. Harris raised his hand. "Dr. Thompson, how do we ensure that our policies and practices are aligned with legal standards?"

"An excellent question, Mr. Harris," Dr. Thompson replied. "Ensuring alignment with legal standards requires a systematic approach to policy development, review, and revision. We'll regularly review and update our policies and procedures to ensure that they reflect changes in legal requirements, emerging best practices, and feedback from stakeholders. By engaging in ongoing monitoring and evaluation, we can identify and address gaps or discrepancies in our compliance efforts, and ensure that our policies and practices remain up-to-date and legally sound."

She clicked to the next slide, which displayed examples of legal compliance frameworks, policy documents, and training materials for educational leaders. "Our approach to ensuring compliance with legal standards will be proactive, systematic, and focused on upholding the integrity and credibility of our educational institution."

Finally, Dr. Thompson emphasized the importance of **Professional Development and Training**. "Professional development and training are essential for ensuring that our staff are knowledgeable about legal requirements and compliant with legal standards," she concluded. "We'll provide regular training sessions, workshops, and resources to equip our staff with the knowledge and skills needed to navigate legal complexities, make informed decisions, and uphold legal standards in their practice. By investing in the professional development of our staff, we can create a culture of compliance and accountability that supports the success and well-being of our students and community."

As the faculty members filed out of the auditorium, Dr. Thompson could sense their growing commitment to ensuring compliance with legal standards. By emphasizing the importance of knowledge of legal requirements, policy development and implementation, alignment with legal standards, and professional development and training, she had equipped her team with the knowledge and tools needed to navigate the complex legal landscape of education with diligence, integrity, and professionalism. She knew that with their collective effort and dedication, they would uphold the highest standards of compliance and ensure the success and well-being of their students and community.

Protecting Student and Staff Rights

Dr. Thompson smoothly transitioned into the next subpoint of her discussion on legal and ethical issues in educational leadership, emphasizing the paramount importance of protecting the rights of students and staff. Assembled once more in the school auditorium, the faculty listened attentively, recognizing the significance of fostering a safe and inclusive environment where all members of the school community are respected and valued.

"Good morning, everyone," Dr. Thompson greeted, her voice infused with empathy and determination. "Today, we address the critical imperative of protecting the rights of our students and staff, ensuring that they are treated with dignity, fairness, and respect in all aspects of their educational experience."

She clicked to the first slide, displaying images depicting students and staff engaging in various educational activities, surrounded by symbols of rights and freedoms. "Protecting student and staff rights is a fundamental responsibility of educational leaders," she began. "It's about upholding the principles of equality, diversity, and inclusion, and ensuring that all members of our school community have the opportunity to learn, work, and thrive in a safe and supportive environment."

Dr. Thompson emphasized the importance of **Respect for Diversity and Inclusion**. "Respect for diversity and inclusion is essential for protecting student and staff rights," she continued. "We'll foster a culture of respect and acceptance that celebrates the diverse identities, backgrounds, and perspectives of our students and staff. By promoting inclusivity and diversity, we can create an environment where everyone feels valued, supported, and empowered to succeed."

She moved on to **Prevention of Discrimination and Harassment**. "Prevention of discrimination and harassment is paramount for protecting student and staff rights," Dr. Thompson explained. "We'll implement clear policies and procedures that prohibit discrimination and harassment based on race, ethnicity, gender, sexual orientation, disability, or any other protected characteristic. We'll provide training and education to staff and students on recognizing and addressing discrimination and harassment, and take prompt and effective action to investigate and address any allegations of misconduct. By fostering a culture of respect and accountability, we can create a safe and inclusive environment where everyone can learn and work free from discrimination and harassment."

Mrs. Lee raised her hand. "Dr. Thompson, how do we ensure

that our efforts to protect student and staff rights are effective and meaningful?"

"An excellent question, Mrs. Lee," Dr. Thompson replied. "Ensuring effective protection of student and staff rights requires a multi-faceted approach that encompasses policy development, training, enforcement, and ongoing monitoring and evaluation. We'll regularly review and update our policies and procedures to ensure that they reflect best practices and legal requirements, provide comprehensive training and education to staff and students on their rights and responsibilities, and establish clear mechanisms for reporting and addressing violations. By fostering a culture of accountability and transparency, we can ensure that our efforts to protect student and staff rights are effective and meaningful."

She clicked to the next slide, which displayed examples of policies and procedures related to diversity, inclusion, discrimination, and harassment, as well as training materials and resources for staff and students. "Our commitment to protecting student and staff rights will be unwavering, as we strive to create a safe, inclusive, and respectful environment where everyone can learn, work, and thrive."

Finally, Dr. Thompson emphasized the importance of **Empowerment and Advocacy**. "Empowerment and advocacy are essential for protecting student and staff rights," she concluded. "We'll empower students and staff to advocate for their rights and speak out against injustice, and provide support and resources to help them navigate challenges and obstacles. By fostering a culture of empowerment and advocacy, we can ensure that everyone in our school community has the opportunity to exercise their rights, have their voices heard, and contribute to positive change."

As the faculty members filed out of the auditorium, Dr. Thompson could sense their renewed commitment to protecting the rights of students and staff. By emphasizing the importance of respect for diversity and inclusion, prevention of discrimination and harassment, effectiveness and meaningfulness of protection efforts, and empowerment and advocacy, she had equipped her team with the knowledge and tools needed to create a safe, inclusive, and respectful environment where everyone can learn, work, and thrive. She knew that with their collective effort and dedication, they would uphold the rights and dignity of every member of their school community, ensuring that their educational institution remained a beacon of equality, justice, and opportunity.

Promoting Ethical Decision-Making

Dr. Thompson gracefully transitioned into the next subpoint of her discussion on legal and ethical issues in educational leadership, emphasizing the crucial importance of promoting ethical decision-making among staff and students. Assembled once more in the school auditorium, the faculty listened attentively, recognizing the significance of fostering a culture of integrity and ethical leadership within their educational community.

"Good afternoon, everyone," Dr. Thompson greeted, her voice filled with conviction and purpose. "Today, we embark on the essential task of promoting ethical decision-making, instilling in our staff and students the values of honesty, fairness, and integrity that are fundamental to ethical leadership."

She clicked to the first slide, displaying images depicting ethical dilemmas, ethical principles, and ethical decision-making frameworks. "Promoting ethical decision-making is a cornerstone of effective educational leadership," she began. "It's about equipping our staff and students with the knowledge, skills, and moral courage needed to navigate complex ethical challenges and make principled decisions that uphold the highest standards of integrity and accountability."

Dr. Thompson emphasized the importance of **Ethical Leadership**. "Ethical leadership sets the tone for our educational community," she continued. "We, as leaders, must model ethical behavior and demonstrate a commitment to honesty, fairness, and transparency in all that we do. By setting a positive example, we can inspire others to follow suit and create a culture of ethical leadership that permeates every aspect of our educational institution."

She moved on to **Ethics Education and Training**. "Ethics education and training are essential for promoting ethical decision-making among staff and students," Dr. Thompson explained. "We'll provide opportunities for staff and students to learn about ethical principles, values, and frameworks, and engage in discussions and activities that challenge their ethical reasoning skills. By fostering a deep understanding of ethics and morality, we can empower our staff and students to make informed and principled decisions in their personal and professional lives."

Mr. Harris raised his hand. "Dr. Thompson, how do we cultivate a culture of ethical decision-making within our educational community?"

"An excellent question, Mr. Harris," Dr. Thompson replied. "Cultivating a culture of ethical decision-making requires a concerted effort to integrate ethics into every aspect of our educational programs and operations. We'll incorporate ethical considerations into curriculum development, instructional practices, and school policies and procedures, and provide opportunities for staff and students to apply ethical principles in real-world situations. By embedding ethics into the fabric of our educational community, we can create a culture where ethical decision-making is valued, practiced, and celebrated."

She clicked to the next slide, which displayed examples of ethics education and training initiatives, ethical leadership practices, and ethical decision-making tools. "Our commitment to promoting ethical decision-making will be unwavering, as we strive to cultivate a culture of integrity, honesty, and accountability within our educational community."

Finally, Dr. Thompson emphasized the importance of **Reflection and Dialogue**. "Reflection and dialogue are essential for promoting ethical decision-making," she concluded. "We'll create opportunities for staff and students to engage in ethical reflection and dialogue, discuss ethical dilemmas and challenges, and explore alternative perspectives and solutions. By fostering open and honest communication, we can create a supportive environment where everyone feels empowered to make ethical decisions and uphold the values of our educational community."

As the faculty members filed out of the auditorium, Dr. Thompson could sense their renewed commitment to promoting ethical decision-making within their educational community. By emphasizing the importance of ethical leadership, ethics education and training, cultivation of a culture of ethical decision-making, and reflection and dialogue, she had equipped her team with the knowledge and tools needed to navigate complex ethical challenges with wisdom, integrity, and compassion. She knew that with their collective effort and dedication, they would create a culture of integrity and ethical leadership that would serve as a beacon of excellence and inspiration for generations to come.

Case Studies of Legal and Ethical Challenges

Dr. Thompson transitioned into the final subpoint of her discussion on legal and ethical issues in educational leadership, presenting real-life case studies of legal and ethical challenges faced by educational institutions. Assembled once more in the school auditorium, the faculty listened intently, eager to learn from the experiences of other organizations and companies.

"Good morning, everyone," Dr. Thompson greeted, her voice carrying a tone of anticipation and reflection. "Today, we explore real-life case studies of legal and ethical challenges encountered by educational institutions, drawing insights from the experiences of organizations and companies facing similar dilemmas."

She clicked to the first slide, displaying images depicting educational institutions and logos of real organizations and companies. "Case studies provide valuable opportunities for learning from the experiences of others," she began. "We'll examine real-life examples of legal and ethical challenges faced by educational institutions, and consider the strategies and lessons learned from these experiences."

Dr. Thompson presented the first case study, focusing on **The College Admissions Scandal**, involving prominent individuals and celebrities bribing college officials to secure admission for their children. "The college admissions scandal raised serious legal and ethical concerns about fairness, integrity, and equity in the college admissions process," she explained. "Educational institutions must have robust policies and procedures in place to prevent fraud and corruption, and ensure that admissions decisions are made based on merit and qualifications."

She moved on to the second case study, highlighting **Data Privacy and Security Breach** at a major university, where sensitive student and faculty information was compromised due to inadequate cybersecurity measures. "Data privacy and security breaches pose significant legal and ethical risks for educational institutions," Dr. Thompson continued. "It's essential for educational leaders to prioritize data privacy and security, implement robust cybersecurity measures, and comply with relevant laws and regulations, such as the Family Educational Rights and Privacy Act (FERPA) and the General Data Protection Regulation (GDPR)."

Mr. Harris raised his hand. "Dr. Thompson, how can educational institutions effectively address these legal and ethical challenges?"

"An excellent question, Mr. Harris," Dr. Thompson replied. "Effectively addressing legal and ethical challenges requires a proactive and multi-faceted approach. Educational institutions must establish clear policies and procedures, provide comprehensive training and education to staff and stakeholders, conduct regular audits and assessments of compliance, and collaborate with legal counsel and experts to navigate complex legal and ethical issues. By prioritizing transparency, accountability, and integrity, educational institutions can mitigate legal and ethical risks and uphold the trust and confidence of their stakeholders."

She clicked to the next slide, which displayed additional case studies and examples of legal and ethical challenges faced by educational institutions. "These case studies offer valuable insights and lessons learned that can inform our approach to navigating legal and ethical challenges in educational leadership."

Finally, Dr. Thompson emphasized the importance of **Continuous Learning and Adaptation**. "Continuous learning and adaptation are essential for effectively addressing legal and ethical challenges," she concluded. "We must remain vigilant, stay informed about emerging issues and best practices, and be willing to adapt our policies and practices in response to changing legal and ethical landscapes. By committing to continuous learning and improvement, we can ensure that our educational institutions remain resilient, ethical, and accountable."

As the faculty members filed out of the auditorium, Dr. Thompson could sense their renewed commitment to addressing legal and ethical challenges in educational leadership. By presenting real-life case studies and examples, she had provided her team with valuable insights and lessons learned that would inform their approach to navigating complex legal and ethical issues. She knew that with their collective effort and dedication, they would uphold the highest standards of integrity, fairness, and accountability, ensuring the success and well-being of their students and community.

10

Chapter 10: Leading Change and Innovation

Principles of Change Management in Education

Dr. Thompson commenced the exploration of Chapter 10, emphasizing the crucial aspect of leading change and innovation in educational institutions. Assembled in the school auditorium, the faculty members anticipated insights into navigating transformative shifts within their educational community.

"Good afternoon, everyone," Dr. Thompson greeted, her voice exuding enthusiasm and determination. "Today, we embark on a journey into the realm of change management and innovation in education, delving into principles that guide successful transformations within our educational institutions."

She clicked to the first slide, displaying images depicting dynamic changes and innovative practices in education. "Change is inevitable in education, and effective change management is essential for fostering growth and progress," she began. "We'll explore principles and strategies that can help us navigate change with agility and resilience, ensuring positive outcomes for our students and community."

Dr. Thompson emphasized the importance of **Vision and Purpose**. "Vision and purpose provide the foundation for successful change initiatives," she continued. "We'll articulate a compelling vision for the future of our educational institution, grounded in our values and aspirations, and communicate it effectively to stakeholders. By rallying around a shared vision, we can inspire commitment, align efforts, and mobilize support for change."

She moved on to **Stakeholder Engagement**. "Stakeholder engagement is critical for successful change management," Dr. Thompson explained. "We'll involve staff, students, parents, and community members in the change process, soliciting their input, addressing their concerns, and empowering them to contribute to the transformation. By fostering collaboration and ownership, we can build momentum and sustain change efforts over time."

Mrs. Lee raised her hand. "Dr. Thompson, how do we ensure that change initiatives are implemented effectively and sustainably?"

"An excellent question, Mrs. Lee," Dr. Thompson replied. "Ensuring effective and sustainable change requires careful planning, execution, and monitoring. We'll develop clear goals and objectives for change initiatives, establish timelines and milestones for implementation, and allocate resources and support as needed. We'll also monitor progress, celebrate successes, and address challenges and obstacles as they arise. By adopting a systematic and iterative approach to change management, we can increase the likelihood of success and create a culture of continuous improvement."

She clicked to the next slide, which displayed examples of successful change initiatives in education, as well as principles and strategies for change management. "Our approach to leading change and innovation will be proactive, collaborative, and focused on creating positive and lasting impact for our students and community."

Finally, Dr. Thompson emphasized the importance of **Adaptability and Resilience**. "Adaptability and resilience are essential qualities for educational leaders," she concluded. "We must be willing to embrace uncertainty, learn from setbacks, and adapt our strategies in response to changing circumstances. By cultivating a growth mindset and fostering a culture of innovation and experimentation, we can position our educational institution for success in an ever-evolving landscape."

As the faculty members filed out of the auditorium, Dr. Thompson could sense their renewed excitement and determination to lead change and innovation within their educational community. By emphasizing the importance of vision and purpose, stakeholder engagement, effective implementation, and adaptability and resilience, she had equipped her team with the knowledge and tools needed to navigate transformative shifts with confidence and purpose. She knew that with their collective effort and dedication, they would lead their educational institution to new heights of excellence and impact, ensuring the success and well-being of their students and community.

Identifying Areas for Innovation

Dr. Thompson seamlessly continued her discourse, delving into the critical task of identifying areas for innovation within educational institutions. Assembled in the school auditorium, the faculty members eagerly anticipated insights into recognizing opportunities for transformative change.

"Good morning, everyone," Dr. Thompson greeted, her voice resonating with anticipation and inspiration. "Now, let us explore the vital process of identifying areas for innovation within our educational ecosystem, where every challenge presents an opportunity for growth and progress."

She clicked to the first slide, unveiling images depicting dynamic educational environments and innovative practices. "Innovation is the engine of progress in education, driving us towards new horizons of excellence and impact," she began. "We'll uncover strategies and approaches that can help us identify areas ripe for innovation, leveraging our collective creativity and expertise to address the evolving needs of our students and community."

Dr. Thompson emphasized the importance of **Data-Informed Decision Making**. "Data-informed decision making is essential for identifying areas for innovation," she continued. "We'll analyze student performance data, feedback from stakeholders, and trends in education to identify areas of need and opportunity. By leveraging data to inform our decision-making process, we can prioritize initiatives that have the greatest potential to positively impact student learning and achievement."

She moved on to **Needs Assessment and Stakeholder Input**. "Needs assessment and stakeholder input are critical for identifying areas for innovation," Dr. Thompson explained. "We'll engage in dialogue with staff, students, parents, and community members to understand their needs, aspirations, and concerns. By soliciting input from stakeholders, we can gain valuable insights into areas where innovation is most needed and most likely to succeed."

Mr. Harris raised his hand. "Dr. Thompson, how do we ensure that our innovation efforts align with the mission and values of our educational institution?"

"An excellent question, Mr. Harris," Dr. Thompson replied. "Ensuring alignment with the mission and values of our educational institution requires us to ground our innovation efforts in our core beliefs and aspirations. We'll conduct a thorough review of our mission, vision, and values, and identify innovation opportunities that align with our overarching goals and priorities. By staying true to our mission and values, we can ensure that our innovation efforts are purposeful, impactful, and sustainable."

She clicked to the next slide, which displayed examples of innovative initiatives in education, as well as strategies for identifying areas for innovation. "Our approach to identifying areas for innovation will be holistic, data-driven, and collaborative, empowering us to unlock the full potential of our educational institution."

Finally, Dr. Thompson emphasized the importance of **Continuous Reflection and Improvement**. "Continuous reflection and improvement are essential for sustaining a culture of innovation," she concluded. "We must regularly evaluate the effectiveness of our innovation efforts, solicit feedback from stakeholders, and adapt our strategies based on lessons learned. By fostering a culture of continuous learning and improvement, we can ensure that our educational institution remains at the forefront of innovation and excellence."

As the faculty members filed out of the auditorium, Dr. Thompson could sense their renewed excitement and commitment to identifying areas for innovation within their educational community. By emphasizing the importance of data-informed decision making, needs assessment and stakeholder input, alignment with mission and values, and continuous reflection and improvement, she had equipped her team with the knowledge and tools needed to drive transformative change and create lasting impact for their students and community. She knew that with their collective effort and dedication, they would lead their educational institution into a future of innovation, excellence, and opportunity.

Developing and Implementing Change Initiatives

Dr. Thompson seamlessly progressed through her discussion, focusing on the pivotal stage of developing and implementing change initiatives within educational institutions. Assembled in the school auditorium, the faculty members eagerly awaited insights into executing transformative strategies with precision and efficacy.

"Good afternoon, everyone," Dr. Thompson greeted, her voice imbued with energy and purpose. "Now, let us delve into the dynamic process of developing and implementing change initiatives, where ideas take flight and aspirations become reality."

She clicked to the first slide, unveiling images depicting collaborative planning sessions and action-oriented endeavors. "Change initiatives are the catalysts for innovation and progress in education," she began. "We'll explore strategies and methodologies that can help us develop and implement change initiatives with clarity, purpose, and impact."

Dr. Thompson emphasized the importance of **Strategic Planning and Goal Setting**. "Strategic planning and goal setting provide the roadmap for change initiatives," she continued. "We'll articulate clear goals and objectives for our initiatives, aligning them with our vision, mission, and values. By establishing a strategic framework, we can ensure that our efforts are focused, coordinated, and effective."

She moved on to **Collaborative Decision Making and Empowerment**. "Collaborative decision making and empowerment are essential for successful change initiatives," Dr. Thompson explained. "We'll engage stakeholders in the planning and implementation process, soliciting their input, leveraging their expertise, and empowering them to take ownership of the change. By fostering a culture of collaboration and empowerment, we can build momentum and ensure that our initiatives are embraced and supported by the entire educational community."

Mrs. Lee raised her hand. "Dr. Thompson, how do we overcome resistance to change and ensure buy-in from stakeholders?"

"An excellent question, Mrs. Lee," Dr. Thompson replied. "Overcoming resistance to change requires us to address concerns, build trust, and communicate effectively with stakeholders. We'll provide opportunities for dialogue and feedback, address misconceptions and fears, and highlight the benefits and opportunities associated with the change. By fostering a culture of transparency, openness, and inclusivity, we can build consensus and ensure that everyone feels heard and valued."

She clicked to the next slide, which displayed examples of change initiatives in education, as well as strategies for developing and implementing change. "Our approach to developing and implementing change initiatives will be collaborative, strategic, and action-oriented, empowering us to drive meaningful transformation within our educational institution."

Finally, Dr. Thompson emphasized the importance of **Monitoring and Evaluation**. "Monitoring and evaluation are essential for ensuring the success and sustainability of change initiatives," she concluded. "We'll track progress, gather feedback, and evaluate outcomes to assess the effectiveness of our initiatives and identify areas for improvement. By embracing a culture of continuous learning and improvement, we can ensure that our change initiatives are impactful, responsive, and adaptive."

As the faculty members filed out of the auditorium, Dr. Thompson could sense their renewed commitment and enthusiasm for developing and implementing change initiatives within their educational community. By emphasizing the importance of strategic planning and goal setting, collaborative decision making and empowerment, overcoming resistance to change, and monitoring and evaluation, she had equipped her team with the knowledge and tools needed to drive transformative change and create lasting impact for their students and community. She knew that with their collective effort and dedication, they would lead their educational institution into a future of innovation, excellence, and opportunity.

Overcoming Resistance to Change

Dr. Thompson seamlessly transitioned into the discussion on overcoming resistance to change, a pivotal aspect of leading transformative initiatives within educational institutions. Gathered once more in the school auditorium, the faculty members eagerly awaited strategies to navigate challenges and foster acceptance of innovation.

"Good morning, everyone," Dr. Thompson greeted, her voice projecting empathy and resolve. "Now, let us explore the complex terrain of overcoming resistance to change, where perseverance and empathy guide us towards collective growth and progress."

She clicked to the first slide, revealing images depicting individuals grappling with uncertainty and adaptation. "Resistance to change is a natural response to uncertainty and disruption," she began. "We'll examine strategies and approaches that can help us address resistance with empathy, resilience, and determination, ensuring that our change initiatives are embraced and supported by all stakeholders."

Dr. Thompson emphasized the importance of **Effective Communication and Transparency**. "Effective communication and transparency are essential for overcoming resistance to change," she continued. "We'll communicate openly and honestly with stakeholders, sharing information about the rationale, goals, and expected outcomes of the change. By fostering a culture of transparency and dialogue, we can build trust and alleviate concerns, empowering stakeholders to embrace the change with confidence and enthusiasm."

She moved on to **Empathy and Active Listening**. "Empathy and active listening are powerful tools for overcoming resistance to change," Dr. Thompson explained. "We'll listen attentively to the concerns and perspectives of stakeholders, acknowledging their fears, frustrations, and uncertainties. By demonstrating empathy and understanding, we can validate their experiences and emotions, fostering trust and collaboration in the change process."

Mr. Harris raised his hand. "Dr. Thompson, how do we address entrenched resistance to change from certain stakeholders?"

"An excellent question, Mr. Harris," Dr. Thompson replied. "Addressing entrenched resistance requires us to engage stakeholders in meaningful dialogue and problem-solving. We'll seek to understand the underlying reasons for their resistance, address misconceptions and fears, and explore potential compromises and solutions. By building relationships and finding common ground, we can overcome barriers to change and build momentum towards shared goals."

She clicked to the next slide, which displayed examples of successful strategies for overcoming resistance to change, as well as principles for effective communication and empathy. "Our approach to overcoming resistance to change will be rooted in empathy, collaboration, and resilience, empowering us to navigate challenges and realize our vision for transformative growth."

Finally, Dr. Thompson emphasized the importance of **Celebrating Progress and Success**. "Celebrating progress and success is essential for sustaining momentum and motivation," she concluded. "We'll acknowledge and celebrate milestones, achievements, and breakthroughs along the way, recognizing the collective efforts and contributions of all stakeholders. By celebrating progress and success, we can inspire confidence, build morale, and reinforce our commitment to change and innovation."

As the faculty members filed out of the auditorium, Dr. Thompson could sense their renewed determination and resilience in overcoming resistance to change within their educational community. By emphasizing the importance of effective communication and transparency, empathy and active listening, addressing entrenched resistance, and celebrating progress and success, she had equipped her team with the knowledge and tools needed to navigate challenges and foster acceptance of innovation. She knew that with their collective effort and dedication, they would lead their educational institution into a future of innovation, excellence, and opportunity.

Evaluating the Impact of Innovations

Dr. Thompson seamlessly transitioned into the discussion on evaluating the impact of innovations, a crucial step in the process of leading transformative change within educational institutions. Assembled once more in the school auditorium, the faculty members eagerly awaited insights into measuring the effectiveness of their initiatives.

"Good afternoon, everyone," Dr. Thompson greeted, her voice carrying a tone of anticipation and reflection. "Now, let us delve into the essential task of evaluating the impact of innovations, where evidence and reflection guide us towards continuous improvement and excellence."

She clicked to the first slide, unveiling images depicting data analysis and reflective practice. "Evaluating the impact of innovations is essential for determining their effectiveness and guiding future decisions and actions," she began. "We'll explore strategies and methodologies that can help us assess the outcomes, strengths, and areas for improvement of our initiatives, ensuring that our efforts are aligned with our goals and priorities."

Dr. Thompson emphasized the importance of **Data Collection and Analysis**. "Data collection and analysis are foundational for evaluating the impact of innovations," she continued. "We'll gather quantitative and qualitative data on key indicators of success, such as student performance, engagement, and satisfaction. By analyzing data systematically, we can gain insights into the effectiveness of our initiatives and identify opportunities for refinement and enhancement."

She moved on to **Stakeholder Feedback and Reflection**. "Stakeholder feedback and reflection are invaluable sources of insight for evaluating the impact of innovations," Dr. Thompson explained. "We'll solicit feedback from staff, students, parents, and community members, seeking their perspectives on the outcomes and experiences of the change. By engaging stakeholders in reflective dialogue, we can gain a deeper understanding of the impact of our initiatives and identify areas for further development."

Mrs. Lee raised her hand. "Dr. Thompson, how do we ensure that our evaluation efforts are comprehensive and meaningful?"

"An excellent question, Mrs. Lee," Dr. Thompson replied. "Ensuring comprehensive and meaningful evaluation requires us to consider multiple perspectives and sources of evidence. We'll use a variety of evaluation methods, including surveys, interviews, observations, and assessments, to capture a holistic view of the impact of our initiatives. By triangulating data from different sources, we can corroborate findings and draw robust conclusions about the effectiveness of our efforts."

She clicked to the next slide, which displayed examples of evaluation frameworks and methodologies, as well as principles for data-driven decision making and reflective practice. "Our approach to evaluating the impact of innovations will be rigorous, evidence-based, and collaborative, empowering us to make informed decisions and drive continuous improvement."

Finally, Dr. Thompson emphasized the importance of **Action Planning and Iteration**. "Action planning and iteration are essential for translating evaluation findings into meaningful change," she concluded. "We'll develop action plans based on evaluation results, outlining specific steps for refining, scaling, or discontinuing initiatives as needed. By embracing a culture of continuous learning and improvement, we can ensure that our educational institution remains responsive, adaptive, and resilient."

As the faculty members filed out of the auditorium, Dr. Thompson could sense their renewed commitment to evaluating the impact of innovations within their educational community. By emphasizing the importance of data collection and analysis, stakeholder feedback and reflection, comprehensive evaluation methods, and action planning and iteration, she had equipped her team with the knowledge and tools needed to drive meaningful change and create lasting impact for their students and community. She knew that with their collective effort and dedication, they would lead their educational institution into a future of innovation, excellence, and opportunity.

Sustaining Long-Term Improvement and Growth

Dr. Thompson seamlessly transitioned into the discussion on sustaining long-term improvement and growth, recognizing the importance of maintaining momentum and progress over time within educational institutions. Gathered once more in the school auditorium, the faculty members eagerly awaited insights into fostering a culture of continuous improvement.

"Good morning, everyone," Dr. Thompson greeted, her voice exuding determination and optimism. "Now, let us explore the critical task of sustaining long-term improvement and growth, where perseverance and dedication lead us towards enduring excellence and impact."

She clicked to the first slide, unveiling images depicting ongoing collaboration and reflection. "Sustaining long-term improvement and growth requires a commitment to continuous learning and adaptation," she began. "We'll examine strategies and approaches that can help us embed a culture of continuous improvement within our educational institution, ensuring that our efforts yield lasting benefits for our students and community."

Dr. Thompson emphasized the importance of **Leadership and Vision**. "Leadership and vision are foundational for sustaining long-term improvement and growth," she continued. "We'll articulate a compelling vision for the future of our educational institution, grounded in our values and aspirations, and champion it with passion and conviction. By providing clear direction and inspiration, we can mobilize support and commitment for sustained improvement and growth."

She moved on to **Professional Learning and Development**. "Professional learning and development are essential for building capacity and expertise within our educational community," Dr. Thompson explained. "We'll invest in ongoing professional development opportunities for staff, empowering them with the knowledge, skills, and resources needed to thrive in a rapidly changing educational landscape. By nurturing a culture of lifelong learning and growth, we can cultivate a community of educators who are empowered to lead and innovate."

Mr. Harris raised his hand. "Dr. Thompson, how do we ensure that our improvement efforts are aligned with the evolving needs of our students and community?"

"An excellent question, Mr. Harris," Dr. Thompson replied. "Ensuring alignment with the evolving needs of our students and community requires us to stay attuned to changing trends, priorities, and aspirations. We'll engage stakeholders in ongoing dialogue and feedback loops, soliciting their input and insights into emerging needs and opportunities. By remaining responsive and adaptive, we can ensure that our improvement efforts are relevant, impactful, and sustainable."

She clicked to the next slide, which displayed examples of successful strategies for sustaining long-term improvement and growth, as well as principles for effective leadership and professional development. "Our approach to sustaining long-term improvement and growth will be rooted in collaboration, innovation, and resilience, empowering us to navigate challenges and seize opportunities with confidence and purpose."

Finally, Dr. Thompson emphasized the importance of **Celebrating Milestones and Successes**. "Celebrating milestones and successes is essential for maintaining morale and motivation," she concluded. "We'll acknowledge and celebrate the progress and achievements of our educational community, recognizing the collective efforts and contributions of all stakeholders. By celebrating our successes, we can inspire confidence, build momentum, and reinforce our commitment to continuous improvement and growth."

As the faculty members filed out of the auditorium, Dr. Thompson could sense their renewed determination and enthusiasm for sustaining long-term improvement and growth within their educational community. By emphasizing the importance of leadership and vision, professional learning and development, alignment with evolving needs, and celebrating milestones and successes, she had equipped her team with the knowledge and tools needed to drive meaningful change and create lasting impact for their students and community. She knew that with their collective effort and dedication, they would lead their educational institution into a future of innovation, excellence, and opportunity.

About the Author

Goodson Mumba is a multifaceted individual known for his diverse expertise and prolific contributions across various fields. As an infopreneur, thought leader, and spiritual leader, he has inspired countless individuals through his insightful teachings and impactful writings. Mumba is also an accomplished author, with several notable works to his name, including "Understanding Corporate Worship," "The Years I Spent in a Week," "Management By Harmony," "The CEO's Diary," "Change to Change" and "Creative Thinking for results" His literary works span topics ranging from business management to personal development and spirituality, reflecting his broad range of interests and insights.

With a Master of Business Leadership (MBL) and a Bachelor of Arts in Theology (BTh), Mumba brings a unique blend of business acumen and spiritual wisdom to his work. His educational background is further enriched by a Group Diploma in Management Studies, providing him with a solid foundation in organizational dynamics and leadership principles. Additionally, Mumba holds diplomas in Education Psychology,

Leadership and Management Styles, Organizational Behaviour, Financial Accounting, Economic Growth and Development, and Project Management, showcasing his commitment to continuous learning and professional development.

Mumba's expertise extends beyond traditional academic disciplines, encompassing areas such as Neuro-Linguistic Programming (NLP) and Positive Psychology. His diverse skill set is complemented by a range of certifications, including Creative Problem Solving and Decision Making, Life Coaching Fundamentals and Techniques, Professional Life Coaching, and Performance Management System Design. These certifications reflect Mumba's dedication to equipping himself with the tools and knowledge necessary to empower others and drive positive change.

As an author, Mumba's writings reflect his deep understanding of human nature, organizational dynamics, and spiritual principles. His works offer practical insights, actionable strategies, and inspirational guidance for individuals seeking personal growth, professional success, and spiritual fulfillment. Mumba's holistic approach to life and leadership resonates with readers worldwide, making him a respected figure in both the business and spiritual communities.

Overall, Goodson Mumba's diverse background, extensive knowledge, and profound insights make him a sought-after speaker, mentor, and author. His commitment to excellence, lifelong learning, and service to others continues to inspire individuals to unlock their full potential and lead lives of purpose and significance.

Goodson Mumba is renowned for initiating the concept of Management by Harmony, revolutionizing traditional management practices with a focus on balanced and holistic approaches. He has authored two influential books on this subject: "Introduction to Management by Harmony" and its sequel, "Management by Harmony."

Mumba's work has significantly impacted the field, offering innovative strategies for fostering organizational harmony and efficiency. His contributions continue to shape contemporary management theories and practices.

www.ingramcontent.com/pod-product-compliance
Lightning Source LLC
Chambersburg PA
CBHW071829210526
45479CB00001B/56